Illustrated **BUYER'S GUIDE**

CLASSIC
HONDA
MOTORCYCLES

BILL SILVER

MBI Publishing Company

First published in 2000 by MBI Publishing Company, 729 Prospect Avenue, PO Box 1, Osceola, WI 54020-0001 USA

MBI Publishing Company books are also available at discounts in bulk quantity for industrial or sales-promotional use. For details write to Special Sales Manager at Motorbooks International Wholesalers & Distributors, 729 Prospect Avenue, PO Box 1, Osceola, WI 54020-0001 USA.

Library of Congress Cataloging-in-Publication Data Available
ISBN 0-7603-0749-0

On the front cover: With its 9500 RPM redline and racy styling, Honda's CB77 Super Hawk helped create Honda's early reputation for building high-performance motorcycles. When equipped with Honda's factory racing parts, the 300cc Super Hawk could top 100 miles per hour, faster than many bikes with over twice its displacement. Today the CB77 Super Hawk is one of the most sought-after classic Hondas. *Photo by Jeff Hackett*

On the back cover: Top: In 1959 Honda stunned the motorcycling world by introducing the CB92 Benly, a 124cc twin-cylinder machine that featured magnesium hubs, a racing-hump seat, and an engine that revved to an astounding 10,500 RPM. Today the CB92 Benly is one of the most valuable early Hondas. *AMA photo* **Bottom:** While it wasn't a huge sales success when new, Honda's CBX is now considered one of the most desirable Hondas to own. *AMA photo*

Designed by Laura Henrichsen

Printed in the United States of America

Contents

Introduction

Soichiro Honda dreamed of creating practical, affordable machines. Every new model he created was a dream fulfilled for Soichiro, beginning with his version of The Model A, which consisted of a surplus generator engine mounted to a bicycle. He even called a number of the early motorcycles Dreams.

A number of his machines also bore the name Benly, which means "convenient" in Japanese. If it wasn't functional, then it wasn't worth producing and selling to the public. So, while styling certainly was a consideration for Soichiro, every product also had to work properly and serve the purpose for which it was intended. At the Honda factory, a prominently posted sign stated, "We are dedicated to supplying products of the highest efficiency at reasonable prices for worldwide customer satisfaction." That credo is responsible for motorcycles honored by their owners all over the world.

Mr. Honda's dynamic legacy has propelled the Honda Motor Company and the Japanese motorcycle industry to worldwide success. Honda's reliable, high-quality motorcycles have become true milestones in motorcycle history. Its use of exotic materials and advanced design has made the Honda name a flagship in transportation, especially in the motorcycle industry. As we review some of the significant models produced, you will see how much creative engineering and comprehensive vision has been applied in the design, production, and function of so many of the varied products of Mr. Honda's brilliant mind.

Soichiro Honda: Dreamer, self-taught engineer, industrialist, founder, and driving force of Honda Motor Company. Born: Nov. 17, 1906, Shizuoka prefecture, Japan; died: Aug. 5, 1991, Tokyo, Japan.

The original site of American Honda Motor Corporation headquarters in the United States was located at 4077 Pico Boulevard, Los Angeles, California.

Honda Timeline

1946 Soichiro Honda establishes Honda Technical Research Institute in Hamamatsu.

1947 Honda releases first product, the A-Type bicycle engine.

1948 Honda Motor Co. Ltd. incorporated.

1949 Honda produces first motorcycle, the Model C (96cc-2 stroke).

1950 Dream D-type (98cc-2 stroke).

1951 Dream E-type released (146cc, 4-cycle).

1953 Benly J produced (90cc, 4-cycle).

1958 C100 Super Cub first sold.

1959 Honda racing team goes to Isle of Man races, capturing a 6th place in the 125cc class. Practice bikes include the 1959 CB92 Benly Super Sport model. American Honda Motor Co. established in Los Angeles, Calif.

1960 Motorcycle production begins at Suzuka Factory; first wet-sump Dreams produced.

1961 Honda releases new line of 250-305cc, wet-sump sports bikes: the Hawk/Super Hawk.

1962 "You meet the nicest people on a Honda" sales campaign introduced in United States—
Honda releases the model CL72, 250cc Scrambler.

1965 New model releases include S90, CB160, CL77, DOHC CB450 Black Bomber.

1966 Honda wins Constructor's Championship in all classes (50cc, 125cc, 250cc, 350cc, and 500cc) at World Grand Prix, an international first.

1969 Honda releases the SOHC CB750, first production transverse, four-cylinder, SOHC machine equipped with standard front disc brake.

1973 Honda reenters the two-stroke racing market with the CR250 Elsinore.

1975 Honda GL1000 Gold Wing released, with water-cooled, flat-four powerplant and shaft-drive.

1978 New transverse, four-valve, pushrod engine twin, the CX500.

1979 Honda CBX, first production transverse six-cylinder, DOHC 1047cc machine and a full line of DOHC four-valve fours from 750 to 1100cc by 1983.

1982 Honda's water-cooled V-4, V45 Sabre released.

1983 First V45 Interceptor introduced.

Chapter 1

Getting Started

The purpose of this book is to outline and highlight the most collectible and practical Honda motorcycles of the 1960s and 1970s as well as some significant 1980s models. The emphasis will be on street bikes, with a nod to the off-road and competition machines. The book begins with the earliest, single-cylinder models, works through the variations of twins, both parallel and some V-configurations, then moves onto the inline fours (and even a six!), and then winds down with the touring machines. Some significant off-road models will be mentioned at the end of the book, but the focus here is primarily on street bikes and classic roadracers.

The book will also acknowledge a few extremely rare and/or single-year models and other bikes of special interest from this period.

Product Codes

A product code is shown as the center three digits in most part numbers, designating the model application. Honda ran through 470 product codes by the time it reached the CX500D in 1980–81. Use of the three-digit product codes identifies the bike and/or the model from which a part originated.

The first all-Honda-designed machine was the 1950 Dream D, featuring a 5.5-horsepower engine and two-speed gearbox. Dream 3E models like this 1953 example were upgraded with three-speed transmissions. In 1953, 32,000 units were produced. Restoration by Jeff Lloyd.

Note the outboard lever pivots in this close-up photo of the speedometer and controls of a 3E model.

Specifically, product code 001 was a Honda C100 Cub and 470 the aforementioned CX500D. Any significant variations of a particular model received their own product codes as well. So, while a C100 Honda Cub started out with an 001 code, the electric-start version became a C102 (003), and the 55cc Trail version was a C105 (002), all with the same basic roots. The majority of the parts of these three models will interchange, but the specifics (i.e. electric-start model or trail model) of each model called for a new product code. From about 1983 on, Honda converted the product codes to a two-letter one-digit sequence, such as the MA2 designation for a 1981–82 CBX. If you're seeking parts or information for your machine, it is wise to be as accurate as possible when describing your particular model. Knowing the product code prevents unnecessary confusion and error at the dealer's parts departments or when negotiating with a private party.

A magneto provided the ignition for the 146-cc overhead-valve, single cylinder engine from a 3E, with generator/battery-powered lighting.

Parts Availability

In 1958, when Honda Motor Company began its marketing of machines to the United States, Mr. Honda promised the North American distributors that his company would always supply parts for any model ever sold in this country. Until his death, he kept that promise, and although the parts availability was pretty thin, once or twice a year a number of rare "backordered" items found their way over to the United States. This was much to the delight of a growing number of dedicated restorers of bikes like the outrageous CB92 Super Sport, sold only from 1960 to 1962 with approximately 1,051 units delivered in the United States.

Despite Honda Motor Company's announcements in the early 1990s about curtailing production of parts for bikes older than 15 years, CB92 footpeg rubbers could still be obtained from American Honda warehouses in 1998. This, however, is an oddity, as the U.S. parts warehouses have been virtually exhausted of any significant pre-1975 motorcycle parts. There does seem to be an occasional exception to the rule, if a part is in continuous demand over the years.

Bear in mind that Honda has produced hundreds of different models of machines, often in colors never seen in the United States. For many years, Honda stocked parts in the colors specified for each application. This became an overwhelming burden on the parts system, as the number of new models continued and as Honda began to build automobiles and had to stock parts for them as well. In the end, Honda could offer many items only in a paintable, gray primer finish in order to reduce the number of items in inventory. So don't be disappointed if you get a NOS CB72 fuel tank in Z-code primer rather than the original Scarlet Red. You'll be lucky to find one at all these days.

Parts Quality

Quality of the replacement parts began to degrade as the demand subsided. Items were being shipped to fill backorders for quantities of 10, 50, or 100, where previous production runs had been for thousands of units. Restorers began to notice that the parts were no longer of the same material, texture, shape, or color of the previously supplied items. Suddenly, it became necessary to have to fit and adjust either your machine or the part just to be able to use it. Die-cast parts were being recast in rough sand castings, with little attention to the original finish. Casting flaws, grinding marks, shoddy chrome-plating, and spray-can finishes became routine.

It would seem reasonable to conclude that these small-run backorders were being sent out to local job-shops, along with the patterns, molds, or blueprints, and filled as economically as possible. Surely, the massive production machinery, which turns out thousands of parts each day, can't be shut down to do a couple of side covers for a CL77. In the end, we had to be thankful for getting something close to what we needed, but many questions remained about Honda's dedication to quality parts.

A glaring example was Honda's decision to re-bend the replacement header pipes for CA/CB 72/77s. Instead of a nice, smooth, continuous curve exiting the exhaust port, there was a short straight section, then an abrupt kink into a straight section of down pipe and another sharp kink

This rare 1954 Japanese-language sales folder features the 220-cc, 8.5-horsepower Dream 4E model. This bike was built in response to the lifting of government-mandated displacement limitations for motorcycles after World War II.

The JC57 Benly first appeared as a 3.8-horsepower 90-cc model in 1953 and grew to a 9.5-horsepower 125-cc model in 1957. The 1954 JA came with rear shocks and a 140-cc engine. The model name changed to JB in 1955. Displacement returned to 125-cc and power output was reduced to 7 horsepower. The 1956 JC57 shown here featured an enclosed chain guard and leading link suspension, and power output was boosted to 8 horsepower. The 1957 JC58 produced 9.5 horsepower and featured oil-damped bottom-link suspension.

to send the remainder rearward. The Super Hawks in particular suffered from this redesign. Often you would see the header pipes contacting the starter motor on both sides as they came down toward the bottom bends. These are made from double-walled tubing, so you just can't throw them in a vise or even a bender and straighten them out a little.

Honda made a similar decision when it replaced the square mirrors with similar ones from a smaller model. There was at least a 30 degree difference in the angle where the stem meets the mirror head, throwing the angle of the mirror up so high that, in many applications, you couldn't even use them. Some brave souls have been able to straighten the angle out, but doing so requires careful support and bending techniques in order to prevent breaking the mirror head or damaging the finish. These are but a couple of examples of what you might find, as you begin to search for those few special parts for your own restoration. Even though they all come from Honda, they are not all the same. So even if you are careful to order the proper part for your particular application, it still may not fit! Caveat emptor!

For most Honda items there is no aftermarket source, although there used to be a few aftermarket suppliers for gaskets, seals, selected electrical components, and even some replacement body parts. Do be aware that some reproduction items floating around may look correct, but on closer inspection, they are obviously not OEM parts.

The 1950 Dream D, Honda's first true complete, in-house effort to build an entire motorcycle, featured a two-stroke engine. *AMA*

A U.S. aftermarket supply company has distributed a combination of overstocked NOS parts, as well as a line of aftermarket replacement parts (often labeled "Superior") for a number of 1960s models (not just Honda parts, either) from C100 to CB77 to CB450. The aftermarket replacements are often stamped "Made in Japan," which was not done to parts made by Honda.

There were also replacement mufflers, which were often fairly accurate copies of the OEM parts, but once you lifted one off of the table, you could tell it was not built to Honda specifications. They probably weigh 30-50 percent less than an original component, for one thing, and often the thin and poorly spot-welded baffles would break loose within a few hours of operation. So, again, buyer beware. Ask plenty of questions about any part that you can't see in the flesh (or metal). The supply of the aftermarket items is almost gone, so this warning is for those of you who might run into a part that looks like an OEM item, but isn't quite up to specs.

If you are just trying to keep your machine functioning, there are other ways to do so. A dying Yazaki speedometer from a 1962 CA77 Dream could be repaired by a local automotive speedometer shop that, perhaps, also does repairs for British bikes. Under the bezels and housings, most speedometers work on similar principles, so any competent repair shop can fix them. Probably the next frontier, for someone looking to provide restoration services, is to create silk-screened speedometer faces for the many machines out there with faded instrument displays. The demand is already there! The same case can be made for accurate seat covers. A few cottage industry shops in Britain have begun to manufacture small lots of certain replacement items, including exhaust headers and chain guards.

The solid brass flywheel housed the points and coils for the magneto ignition and charging system. *Doyne Bruner collection*

This unrestored 1950 Dream D shows the forward-facing carburetor and rear-exit exhaust system. *Doyne Bruner collection*

Getting Help

Networking with other enthusiasts through national or worldwide organizations is an important step in finding the parts or bikes you desire. The Vintage Japanese Motorcycle Club (VJMC) has branches located in the United States (in conjunction with Canada), England, Australia, and New Zealand. There are Classic Honda Clubs in Norway, Sweden, Finland, and other parts of Europe. The Classic Japanese Motorcycle Club (CJMC), located in Northern California, is another American resource.

Sometimes the best way to obtain the parts you need is to buy some "parts bikes." You can resell the remaining carcasses or part them out completely and sell the items bit by bit. Be sure that the parts bike you buy is of the same series as the one you need though! Match the serial numbers of the engine and frames against what you need. Obtaining a copy of a factory parts list is imperative if you want to minimize your time and money expenditures. Honda made a practice of changing anything that was weak or not functioning to its full potential, thus you will often find changes in parts specifications in the middle of a model year. If you pay attention to this warning, your restoration progress and budget will not suffer needlessly.

The Internet is a fast and inexpensive way to locate parts, information, and other restoration assistance. There are huge numbers of newsgroups and subscription lists that specialize in almost anything you can imagine.

Close-up of early Mercury-like Honda Dream logo.
Doyne Bruner collection

A kick starter was a new feature for Honda-powered products, replacing the previous pedals of the earlier machines. *Doyne Bruner collection*

Literature

Honda sales literature dates back to some of the first models. Included in this book is a piece of sales literature for a 1954 Dream 4E. There was an advertising blitz in many motorcycle magazines, such as *Cycle* and *Motorcyclist*, beginning in 1959, when the CE71 and Honda 50 Cubs were being shipped to new dealers in the United States. Sales brochures often covered several related machines, like the full complement of Cubs or a Benly 150, in conjunction with a CB92 Benly Super Sport. In 1962, for example, Honda released a "full-line" sales sheet, covering the 50cc Cub series, 125cc Benly Super Sport, 150 Benly, 250 Dream, and Hawk, as well as the 305 Dream and Super Hawk bikes. Also included was a photo of the Juno scooter, which was never sold here.

In order for the dealers to be able to service these new machines, Honda produced full-page parts books, showing exploded views of each system. It also supplied comprehensive shop manuals, detailing the theory of design, as well as the appropriate service procedures for each model. The translations from Japanese into English, in the owners and service manuals, were rather cryptic and in some cases nonsensical. The 1959–60 CB92 owners manuals detailed how to gain the top speed through use of the "flying posture," where one was to extend oneself rearward in a fully prone position, while attempting to achieve the advertised 81 miles per hour mark. Color brochures showing factory riders lying prone on 250-305 Dreams were distributed in 1959–60.

Motorcycle pioneer Floyd Clymer created a line of aftermarket service manuals for almost all models of Hondas. His early 250-305 shop manual was a combination of the two existing Honda factory service manuals for those models. The first factory shop manuals for the wet-sump models consisted of a 1961 Dream/Super Hawk edition, followed by a separate CL72 Scrambler manual in 1962. There never was a separate issue for the CL77 Scramblers, however. Clymer's manuals are still in print for most all of the Vintage 1960s-80s Honda models.

Honda's suspension design has improved dramatically since the company built this Dream in 1950. *Doyne Bruner collection*

Throughout the 1960s, as each new model came out, the accompanying service data and owners manuals became more polished and easier to understand. The results were a combination of suggestions from American Honda employees and lots of practice due to the volume of materials that they were producing each year. Not only were they trying to keep up with the volume of bikes being sold to the English-speaking market, but Honda had made inroads into Europe and Scandinavian countries as well and thus needed to produce materials in those languages too. So if you find yourself with a new acquisition vintage Honda, don't be too concerned about finding parts and sales literature, because it is out there, in either original or copy format.

If you are going to own any model Honda, it is necessary to obtain a parts book for reference. Honda continues to release microfiche parts lists for most models, and you can obtain copies of Honda parts lists through the vintage clubs around the world, usually at a reasonable cost. Supplying your local Honda parts department with either a Honda code or the three-part Honda NPS (New Part Number System) will greatly aid the possibility of ordering and securing correct OEM items. Many dealership employees are younger than these machines and they sometimes have little concern or even a reference point for assisting you. If you want to get into their good graces, have the correct part numbers ahead of time.

If you just want to collect literature, you can begin most cheaply by finding motorcycle magazines dating from the late 1950s and the early 1960s. Also, magazines including *Look* and *Life* featured Honda ads as well. Motorcycle swap meets are a source of a lot of sales and service literature, in addition to parts. If you are connected to the Internet, you can locate all kinds of motorcycle literature from dealers who specialize in it.

Placing want ads in the many free classified ad sites will put your request before the eyes of thousands of fellow enthusiasts around the world. Even if you can't get some of the originals, it should be easy to connect with people in other countries who would be able to do color scans or copies of sales literature in their native languages. CB92 advertisements alone have been seen in at least five languages that I'm aware of. The passion of owning and riding motorcycles is a global desire, so it's an opportunity to get some culture and have fun at the same time!

This poster shows the full 1965 Honda motorcycle lineup of future classics, incorporating a reference to their highly successful racing program.

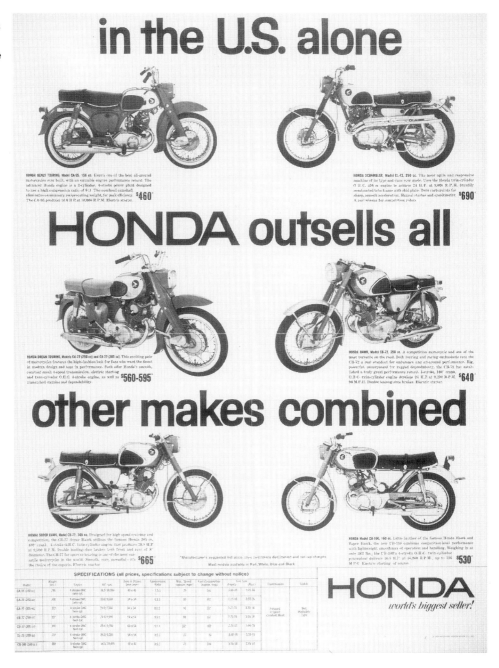

...and top performer in world competition

Honda's superiority is a matter of record. Check the results of competitive events the world over and you'll find Honda out in front. They win. They set records. The 1962 International Grand Prix Championship was a clean sweep for Honda. No other machine can match the tooled perfection of a Honda, whatever the model. Precise as a Swiss watch, yet rugged as a rhino, Honda sets the standard for craftsmanship wherever motorcycles are on their own. Honda gives you the finest motorcycles in the world (at a reasonable price). You'll find six handsome models on the next page. Choose a Champ. Choose a Honda.

Accessories

For most models, Honda made many accessory parts available through dealerships. For the CB72-77, CB92, and C110 machines, Y racing parts were available as separate items or in made-up kits in the case of the Super Hawks. Almost 100 different items were made for the CB72-77s alone. You could get a racing seat, clip-on handlebars (with racing fork bridge, which had no handlebar mounts cast in), hydraulic steering damper components, and extended shifter rods to allow the pegs to be moved further back. There were also alloy rims, two different types of megaphones, racing cams and valve springs, carburetor "air funnels," alloy rear fenders, and a set of number plate brackets for front and rear and all of the special fasteners to assist in the installation.

CL72s had a short list of Y option parts, but it did include an alloy copy of the original fuel tank, complete with holes for the tank badges and brackets for the kneepads. Other than the quick-release gas cap, a painted Y tank looked just like the steel versions.

CB92s got a similar treatment, if you didn't get the full racing kit installed from the factory as a CB92R model. That model included high-compression pistons (requiring side-gap plugs), high-output "red-wire" ignition coils, megaphones in two lengths, racing seat, and a wiring harness and timing kit to remove the charging system altogether, allowing the bike to run in a "total-loss" mode. There were special racing suspension springs and shocks, CR71-derived footpeg assemblies, and alloy

Honda's fantastic racing program was in full swing by 1965, with Hondas competing successfully in almost all GP racing classes.

rim options, as well. Even the nuts and bolts could be specified with holes predrilled for safety wiring.

The little 50cc C110 Sports Cub also got in on the deal with a racing seat, megaphone muffler (either low- or high-mounted), a wild-looking, high-compression piston, and special valve springs, along with a special two-piece crankcase breather set that used the dipstick hole as a source.

Not all Y parts were racing parts, however. The designation of Y was "accessory part," so it applied to other nonracing items as well. Thus, a set of crashbars or a rear luggage rack could be considered a Y part to Honda. Most of that period's Y part numbers ended in –810 suffixes. For example, the standard CB72 footpeg in Japan was a solid, nonfolding item, whereas the folding, U.S.-spec footpeg assy was designated an –810 Y part, even though they were standard issue for all CB72-77s sold in the U.S. during that era. Certainly, a folding footpeg is an asset when racing, but most U.S. riders have come to expect folding footpegs for everyday riding.

Even though the standard Cubs, Benlys, and 250-305 Dreams weren't racing material, they had their own Y parts in the form of fender guards and wing ornaments, as well as crashbars and luggage racks. Honda had a full line of saddlebags, windshields, and even a set of "water-heated" handgrips, kneepads, and seats shown in an early parts manual.

Honda accessory catalogs show lots of Honda trademarked "doo-dads," ranging from pennants to ashtrays to pens and a host of other novelty items. Look for items like these in vintage motorcycle publications classifieds and on-line auction houses. Honda-trademarked memorabilia is getting to be pretty hot property now, so if you see any for sale, buy it!

How Do I Get Started?

Well, buying this book was a good first move! Usually, most vintage Honda enthusiasts already have one or more models in mind, based on their personal experience or the styling of a particular machine. Of course, your budget and level of mechanical skill will play a part in the selection process. For the purpose of this publication, I will assume that you have never considered the purchase of a vintage Honda before you picked up this book. Therefore, I will use all of my own knowledge and experience, as well as that which I have acquired from my friends, acquaintances, and industry contacts, to present a balanced view of Honda motorcycles as a collectible form of transportation.

Next, place ads, network with other vintage enthusiasts, subscribe to vintage clubs, harass your local Honda dealer for leads, go to garage sales, search the Internet and local weekly motorcycle classified ad publications, and so on to find your bike. Your geographic location may hinder or help your cause, to the extent that each region is more likely to have a certain flavor of bikes; and the region also affects the overall condition in which you will find them. Midwest and Northern state areas are restricted by a shorter riding season than in the Southwest, thus you may find more low-mile bikes there. If the bikes are stored in a barn or unheated garage for the winter, they may suffer more from condensation damage internally and weathering externally, in contrast to bikes found in some areas of Arizona or New Mexico, where the air tends to be less humid.

Transporting a Bike

Consider the potential costs of transportation, if your dream bike is located several thousand miles away. Often the cost of transport is equal to or greater than the value of the machine, especially for parts bikes and basket cases. But if you find that one-in-a-thousand perfect match for your needs, then just bite the bullet and go for it. A few hundred dollars shouldn't keep you from acquiring that bike you've been searching for, anyway. There are a number of services that offer safe, affordable bike transportation, but shop around for the best price and go with someone who is reputable and is bonded or can insure your bike for the full replacement value.

Insurance

Unless you plan only to restore and show your bike, you will need to obtain insurance in order to operate it on public roads. Basic liability insurance can be obtained for less than $100 a year for many older machines. Most automobile insurance companies don't want anything to do with a motorcycle, so you will probably have to go to a specialty company. Getting an appraised value for your beloved two-wheeler is another story, and if you have an accident with your prize, you will have a tough time explaining why a fully restored CA95 Benly is now worth $2,500, when it cost about $600 new in the early 1960s. Document your restoration or purchase carefully, just in case the unthinkable happens.

Evaluating a Bike

Once you've committed to a particular model type and have located one, you will need to evaluate its condition as much as possible. For just the CB77 alone, there are at least 1,044 different part numbers, so there is a lot to consider when you decide to buy or not to buy. Make at least a basic checklist—one that covers the main parts, systems, and aspects of the bike—then rough out what your expenditures might be (then figure 100 percent higher than what your highest best guess is) and see if it meets your selection criteria.

For example:

Originality: Is it a complete, intact, OEM-equipped machine? Did someone change the handlebars? The seat? The mufflers? Accessories added? Again, use of an applicable parts book will allow you to evaluate the originality more accurately.

Engine: Is it complete? Any history of repairs? Does it turn over? If not, you need to reconsider this purchase very carefully! If so, does it have good compression? How much is good? It should be 150 to 175 psi, in most cases. Is there damage from accidents or improper maintenance (broken fins, damaged covers or side cases)? Are all of the engine electrics present and functioning? Is the fuel system (petcock, carburetors, and control cables) complete, and was the bike stored properly (either with a full tank of gas with stabilizer, or drained and oil coated), carburetors drained, oil changed, turned over periodically, and so on? Is the clutch stuck (plates stuck together)? Does it shift gears? What does the oil look and smell like? Is it dirty or contaminated with water? Burnt smelling?

Chassis: Does the bike have any accident damage? Are the wheels round and true? Do the brakes and controls work properly? (Check for brake shoes corroded into the hubs and/or sticking front brake calipers on disc-brake models.) Forks bent? Rear swingarm loose or bent? Shocks: OEM or replacements? Frame damage or corrosion? Does it have intact, uncut, undamaged fenders? What is the condition of the seat cover and foam? What is the condition of any chrome or polished parts or painted parts? Is the paint original?

Controls and instrumentation: Are all of the cables and control levers operational? Are the instruments operational (how many miles indicated)?

Electrical: Are all the lights present and functional? Does the charging system work? Are the ignition and handlebar switches, regulators, rectifiers, solenoids, and other lighting controls working? Do you have the keys?

Paperwork: Is there a current title (in the owner's name)? Registration? License plate? Are there back fees and penalties due? Is the bike free of liens?

This is just a rough guide to assist you in asking some pertinent questions about your prospective purchase. Feel free to add an additional 100 questions to this list!

Identifying the Year and Model

Because so many of the "classic" Honda 250-305 twins are still being sought after and restored, here's some information pertinent to this series of machines.

1960s 250–305cc Twins

Often, when you discover a vintage Honda 250 or 305cc twin available for sale, it is lacking the title or other necessary documentation. Depending on the county, state, or country requirements, you will find it necessary to "create" some paperwork for registration purposes. The first step in this process is to determine the correct year of production.

On early 1960s Honda 250-305cc twins, you can pinpoint this information quite accurately, using the frame/engine serial numbers found at various locations on the bike. You will notice that Honda's serial numbers carry a letter (or two), followed by a number (e.g., C77, CA77, CB72, CL77). The "70-72" designation (as in CB72) denotes 250cc models, while the "75-78" designation signifies 305cc models (for instance, CL77). All pre-1961 (C70-71 and C75-76) engines were dry-sump design (separate oil tank). After 1960, the C/CB/CL 72/77-

This 1967 magazine ad highlights the last of the CL77s, with a background illustration reference to the "Honda Custom Group," which referred to add-on kits for the C100 and CM91. (The Rally kit is shown.)

The Honda Custom Group. You take your pick of customized Hondas at your dealer's. Like the Rally here. These models feature a special type of tank, pipe, handlebars, seat. Ride off on your personalized Honda. Wild.

Honda shapes the world of wheels You wonder how they do it. 20 models so cool and calculating. Any one of 'em would make an ideal companion. Low upkeep. Faithful service. Spectacular performance. That famous Honda four-stroke engine won five out of five '66 Grand Prix Championships. 50cc to 500cc. A world's record. That's Honda's bag. You've got to respect it. See your Honda dealer for a safety demonstration ride.

HONDA

You meet the nicest people on a Honda.

series engines were all of conventional wet-sump design (all oil carried within the engine).

Note: When "A" is shown after "C," it is usually a "U.S.-Spec" model. Think "A" for "America."

Engine/Frame Designation Chart

C71–76 (dry sump), C72-77 (wet sump): 250, 305cc (Dream), all had single carburetors

CA72–77/CE71: U.S.-spec versions of touring style machines (Dream)

CS77: 305cc Dream Sport, featuring high-mounted exhaust pipes and mufflers

CB72–77: 250–305cc Super Sport models (dual carburetors)

CL72–77: 250–305cc Scrambler models (dual carburetors)

CR72–77: 250–305cc factory-produced, production roadracers, sold in limited numbers

RC-series: Factory team racers, not for sale

Frame Characteristics:

CA, CE, or CS: Dream models with stamped, sheet-metal frames, forks, and swingers. These models ride on 16-inch wheels (except some CE71s). They are all equipped with twin-shock, leading-link front suspension.

CB and CL: Super Sport/Scrambler models feature tubular-type frames and swingers, fitted with 18-inch (CB) or 19-inch (CL) wheels and conventional, telescopic-style, hydraulic-damped front forks.

CR: These rare 250-305cc (CR72-77) four-stroke, twin-cylinder, production roadracing models were built in 1962. All have double overhead cams (DOHC), four-valve heads, five-speed transmissions, twin double leading shoe (DLS) magnesium front brakes, open megaphone exhaust pipes, and 18-inch wheels, featuring alloy rims. The CR72 and CR77 models were built in very small quantities and few exist in the United States. Only one bike is known to be actively raced in the United States at present. The CR designation was revived in 1973 for the CR250M Elsinore.

There were a few, extremely rare "street-bike" versions of the CR110 (50cc) and CR93 (125cc) production roadracing models, with full lighting systems and muffled exhausts. Probably less than 50 of each of these were ever produced and they were never sold through Honda dealerships in the U.S.

Displacement Code Chart

The chart below shows a few examples of the relationship between the model designation and displacement size of the engine.

Model/Displacement

C(A) Cub-series100/102/110=50cc; 105=55cc

C(A or T)200=Touring 90/Trail 90

C/CA/92=125cc/95=150cc Benly

C/CA72=250cc Dream

C/CA/CS77=305cc Dream

CB92=125cc Benly SS

CB72=250cc Hawk
CB77=305 Super Hawk
CL72=250cc/CL77=305cc Scrambler
CR110=50cc/CR93= 125cc/CR72=250cc/CR77=305cc

Identifying the Year Model from the Serial Numbers

For 250-305cc bikes, built before 1965, the identifying process is relatively easy. In the late 1950s and early 1960s, the year was often coded within the serial number (e.g., C71 59 12345); the center numbers denoting the year (in this case 1959). Later, the first digit of the five-digit frame (and six-digit engine) number was used as the year code (e.g., CB72-11123; a 1961 250cc Sports model).

Here's an overview of the three most popular models and how to tell the dates of manufacture:

CB models: The CB72/77-series (known as 250 Hawks or 305 Super Hawks) were numbered as follows: In 1961–63, the first digit in frame (five digits in 1961–62 and six digits in 1963) and engine serial number (all six digits) was year of manufacture. In 1964, frames and engines both started with 100001 (both six digits). The 1965 models started with 1000001 (seven digit frame and engine numbers) and continued in that fashion. Generally, the frame and engine numbers are within 150 numbers of each other or less.

CB Models

Year	Frame No. beginning	Engine No. beginning
1961	CB77-10001	CB77E-11001
1962	CB77-20001	CB77E-21001
1963	CB77-300001	CB77E-310001
1964*	CB77-100001	CB77E-100001
1964 cont.*	CB77-400001	CB77E-400001
1965–1967	CB77-1000001	CB77E-1000001

* In 1964, two different serial number sequences were offered within the same year.

For CB models, there are several model variations, other than the "regular" Hawk/Super Hawk versions. Apparently, some 1964 models with 400001 serial numbers may be found with Type 2 (360 degree crank) engines or they may have been models destined for the German market (modified to meet special noise restrictions). The rest of the 100001-on (1964) series bikes all seem to be normal Type 1 (180 degree crank) engine versions, however. Then, you may also find the odd CP77 frame/engine, which may or may not be a Police version (usually called a CYP77), as well as a CBM72, which has high bars, turn signals, and a Type 2 (360 degree) crankshaft.

There are also "domestic" versions of CB77s with Type 2 engines. Deviations from the normal numbering sequence usually denote models for specific countries or special applications. Genuine CYP77 Police bikes are all white and have a single, round speedometer, rather than the oval, dual speedo/tachometer gauges of the other models. Some early-model Police bikes had 17-inch wheels, front and rear. Actual Police versions have crash bars, turn signals, solo seats, a rear rack, special lever brackets for the siren controls, patrol lights, and a screaming, cable-driven siren (driven off the rear wheel).

There is no definitive break between years 1965, 1966, and 1967. However, CB77s with Type 2 alloy front forks began at CB77-1030130 and seem to be the beginning of the 1966 models. The chrome-fender CB models, with the "oval" taillight, were introduced from frame number 1056084 and onwards, which was at the end of the production run in 1967 (CB77-1056432 was the last machine). There are three different crankshafts, three transmissions, two series of pistons, three series of camshafts, four different speedometers (running in two different directions), two types of Type 1 (steel) and one Type 2 (alloy) fork assemblies, and three different fork crowns, for the CB-series bikes. This is why you must always check your engine and frame numbers before ordering parts!

Sometimes, the original CB engines have been swapped with other CB or sometimes CL engines. CL engines are not equipped with electric starters but can be retrofitted with CB or CA starter motors and starter clutches, for CB installations. Again, check those serial numbers carefully if you are ordering parts or doing a "correct" ground-up restoration.

CL72 models: CL72s (250 Scramblers) were made from 1962 to 1966. 1962 bikes had five-digit serial numbers (frame) and six-digit engine numbers. Again, the first digit in the five-digit series (six digits in 1963) is the year of manufacture. Thus, a CL72-21977 (example) is a 1962 model. It got confusing in 1964, with an early bike series starting with CL72-1100001 through 1109459, followed by CL72-4000001-4003437 (Type 2 engine or German-market bikes, perhaps?) series. CL72-1000001 and up numbers (all seven digit) were 1965-66 models. CL72 models made after CL72-1008851 had alloy Type 2 forks, "Big" brakes, steel fenders, and were made in late 1965.

IT'S NOT A MOTORCYCLE — NOT A SCOOTER — IT'S AMERICA'S FAVORITE NEW RIDING HABIT!

Whoever you are: workingman, housewife, or student... Wherever you go: to work, to market, or to school... you'll find the perfect answer with a HONDA "50".

For the HONDA "50" is the ultimate in economy, convenience and dependability. You can park it anywhere. It's safer than a bike. It cruises all day at a whisper-quiet 40 miles an hour. It delivers up to 225 miles on a gallon of pump gas! Electric starter optional.

See it and try it today. You'll love **everything** about the HONDA "50". And you'll know why more than one million HONDA "50's" were sold last year alone!

It's for everyone! The Thrifty, Nifty Honda 50 sales brochure extolled the virtues of the Honda "50" Mark 100. Two hundred twenty-five miles per gallon, electric-starting option (C102 electric start model shown), 40 miles per hour, and "safer than a bike" were all selling points for the early models.

Year	CL Models	Frame No. beginning	Engine No. beginning
1962	CL72	CL72-20001	CL72E-210001
1963	CL72	CL72-300001	CL72E-310001
1964	CL72	CL72-1100001	CL72E-1100001
1964 cont.*	CL72	CL72-4000001	CL72E-4000001
1965-on	CL72	CL72-1000001	CL72E-1000001

* In 1964, two different serial number sequences were offered within the same year.

All 250 Scramblers, built through CL72-1107409, have "double-eye" (top and bottom) shocks and a matching swingarm. Shocks with clevis-type ends on the bottom were used, thereafter, on the CL72s and on all CL77 models. The slip-on exhaust silencer seems to have been introduced with 1965 models. There are at least four sets of exhaust pipes/mufflers for the CL72/77-series machines.

The CL77s: The early 305 Scrambler models, CL77-1000001 to 1014495, were built as the original 1965 models and were equipped with CL72-style steel forks and the same "small" 7-inch single leading shoe (SLS) brakes. Bikes after CL77-1014495 had alloy fork sliders, 8-inch DLS brakes, similar to the CB77, but the front wheel is mostly derived from CB450 parts. The chrome fender bikes with the "oval" taillight started production from CL77-1043098 (generally 1967 models). More than 68,240 CL77s were produced.

C/CA Dreams: Most of the information on C/CA72/77s (again 250-305cc) follows the same pattern as the CB series. Of course, all C/CA engines are Type 2 (360 degree crank) engines. While Dream frames often seem to have no serial numbers, they are normally found in a location on the left side of the frame, behind the engine, below the swingarm pivot, and next to (sometimes under) the footpeg mounting bracket. It is an obscured area, often covered with grease and dirt. Models from 1961 and early 1962 have different, more-sculpted styling on the tank and chrome side panels, as well as myriad other smaller details concerning the handlebars, cables, fenders, seats, plastic side covers, and so on.

Note: many 1964 and later U.S. CA77s are stamped CA78, but the engines are all marked CA77. All Dreams, through late 1965 (CA77-1010863), used a tall, thin, wide 12v battery (6v on early dry-sump models, though), which was then superseded by the CB72/77 battery. This change caused the creation of all new parts for the frame, side cover, and tool tray.

Total U.S. Sales

From AHMC records, these are the total U.S. sales for each 250-305 model:

CA72, 1960–67: 5,052
CA77, 1960–69: 61,133
CB72, 1961–66: 3,479
CB77, 1961–69: 72,396
CL72, 1962–65: 10,071
CL77, 1965–68: 66,757
Total: 218,888 units

Turn Signals

Almost all of these 250-305 models sold outside of the United States had factory-installed turn signals (winkers). There are several different versions of turn signals, which correspond to the

Year	Model	Engine	Frame
1960	C72	C72E-010001–034078	C72-10001–34078
	CA72	C72E-A10001–NA	C72-A10001NA
	C77	C77E-010001–011980	C77-10001–11980
	CA77	C77E-A10001–NA	C77-A10001–NA
1961	C72	C72E-1100001–1143976	C72-100001–143960
	CA72	CA72E-110001–110150	CA72-10001–10150
	C77	C77E-110001–111979	C77-10001–11980
	CA77	CA77E-110001–111400	CA77-10001–11980
1962	CA72	CA72E-210001–21025	CA72-20001–20250
	C77	C77E-210001–210520	C77-20001–20520
	CA77	CA77E-210001–210850	CA77-20001–20851
1963	CII72	C72E-310001–349404	C72-340001–352302
	CA72	CA72E-310001–311910	CA72-310001–311910
	C77	C77E-310001–310896	C77-310001–310896
	CA77	CA77E-310001–314731	CA77-310001–314731
1964(1)	CIIIA72	CA72E-100001–100760	CA72-100001–100760
	C78	C77E-100001–101512	C78-100001–101512
	CA78	CA77E-100001–108176	CA78-100001–108176
1964 (2)	CIIIA72	CA72-40000–401542	CA72-400001–401520
	C78	C77E-400001–400978	C78-400001–400975
	CA78	CA77E-400001–403456	CA78-400001–403456
1965-on	CIIIA72	CA72E-1000001–NA	CA72-1000001–NA
	CA78	CA77E-1000001–NA	CA78-1000001–NA

legal requirements of different countries. Because many vintage Hondas came into the country via U.S. servicemen, you might find some bikes equipped with turn signals. But, remember that until 1968, Honda did not equip their U.S.-spec machines with turn signals.

After 1967

Sometimes, you will find 250-305 models registered as 1968–69 models, but keep in mind that they ceased production in 1967 to make way for the CB/CL 250-350 models introduced in 1968. There were left-over bikes in warehouses for several years after the end of production, thus the reason for the post-1967 title/registration paperwork. In many states, the year of sale was the year of the bike, so don't always use the "year" date shown on the title as a guide for buying parts for your machine.

Wiring Harness Tags

The final way to discern the year model of complete, original bikes (that haven't had a wiring harness fire, modification, or some similar misfortune) is to check the main wiring harness between the steering head and the battery connectors (usually somewhere under the fuel tank) for a small white tag attached to the outside of the harness wrapping. It will usually show the part number of the harness, often including the model and the date. Bear in mind that this is the date of manufacture of the harness, not the motorcycle, but almost always corresponds to the date of the bike too.

Identifying 1968 and Later Models

For "next-generation" machines, from 1968 to 69 (175, 350, 750s), Honda began to apply U.S. D.O.T. (Department of Transportation) labels to the steering heads, which are identified as U.S.-spec models. In 1969 labels first showed some required statements about the model being made to U.S. safety standards, but didn't show an actual production date. From 1970 and onwards, all street bikes had an identification label plate attached (usually riveted) to the right side of the steering head, opposite the stamped numbers on the left. This label shows the production date by month and year. In many cases, the *Honda Identification Guide* is of great value, showing the model and highlighting some of the distinctive features. Copies of this 1988 edition guide have gotten scarce and there is now an updated 1999 version. The first edition book covered all Honda models imported and sold in the United States. from 1958 to 1988.

In 1968, Honda began to earmark each successive year's models with a "K" designation. For example, the CB/CL350s, introduced in 1968, were called CB/CL350K0 and each one afterward became K1, K2, K3, and so on. This system was used until 1976, when the models just gained the appropriate year, as in CB550K '76, where the previous 1975 model was a CB550K1. This identification procedure carried on through the late 1980s.

As a last resort, copies of parts booklets (from before the days of microfiche) will guide you in the right direction, with illustrations and listings of serial number changes when a part was changed. By 1968, bikes were being designated as K0, K1, K2 models and each new year had some cosmetic characteristic, which denoted a particular model year. The OEM parts books will be invaluable in your search for parts.

Chapter 2

The Street Singles (1959–90)

When Honda first entered the war-torn motorcycle market of 1948, it began with simple, single-cylinder machines. The first Honda-designed bikes were two-stroke singles with adapted surplus radio generator engines attached to bicycle frames. The Dream E model of 1951 was the first four-stroke machine, a 146cc pushrod design, rated at 5.5 horsepower and weighing in at 213 pounds. By 1958, however, the economical, 50cc C100 Honda Super Cubs were rolling off the assembly line by the hundreds at the Suzuka factory. Its tiny-but-efficient pushrod engine made 4.3 horsepower and the whole machine weighed a scant 121 pounds. Honda followed with an electric-starting version for the ladies, as well as the Sports Cub models, which were capable of 53 miles per hour. Once these bikes established Honda's presence in the motorcycle industry, the company expanded

The first C100s were released in 1959 and were produced by the millions throughout the 1960s. C100s like this 1963 example were capable of 45 miles per hour and 200 miles per gallon. Other variations were the electric-start C102 and the 55-cc C105T trail bike. This was the bike that started it all in the United States. *AMA*

This 1964 C100 was one of 101,106 sold in the United States over a 10-year period. *Troyce Walls collection*

and released larger-capacity machines as the demand for larger displacement models grew at home and abroad.

You Meet the Nicest People on a Honda

This simple but immensely popular slogan, launched in 1962, was one of the most effective motorcycle sales campaigns ever. Although some 250cc bikes (CE71 Dream Sport and some C/CS 71/76 Dreams) were brought in at the beginning of the 1958–59 sales introductions, the emphasis of the sales campaign was on the C100 50cc Honda Cub step-through series machines. Light and affordable at under $250 each, the basic Super Cub was a marvel of efficiency (claiming 200+ miles per gallon) and simplicity, featuring a three-speed transmission with automatic clutch. The tiny 49cc pushrod engine could somehow reach engine speeds of 10,000 rpm and it didn't even have an oil pump. Super Cubs could carry two; and a solo rider could see about 45 miles per hour. If kick-starting was too ungraceful for the ladies, there was a CA102 version with electric-starting. The 55cc version, called the C105T, was configured for trail riding, the ancestor to the legendary Trail 90. From 1962 on, the U.S. version Super Cubs were simply called CA100 Honda 50.

C110 Super Sports Cub and CA110 Sport 50 (1960–69)

If speed was your thing as a youngster (isn't it always?), these little bikes offered the look and feel of a real motorcycle with the gas tank between your knees and a manual clutch with four-speed transmission.

YOU MEET THE NICEST PEOPLE ON A HONDA

Honda changed the image of motorcycling with its "You meet the nicest people" campaign. Imagine what Honda's legal department would think of an ad today showing a small child riding on the luggage rack!

Riding a Cub 50

Riding Cub 50s is a unique experience. The three-speed auto clutch combo of the step-through C100/102/105 Cubs is convenient but challenging to drive in today's traffic. Apparently Honda felt that in most cases the bike could be launched in second gear and then just shifted once into third. If you are not in a hurry and are riding solo on a flat surface, this will move you in a forward direction, albeit at a snail's pace. In order to select first, you have to shift through neutral, which is inconveniently located between first and second. Neutral has a positive stop, so you are forced to double shift from first to neutral and finally to second. Shifting down to first from second requires the same drill. Keeping track of when to single shift and when to double-shift gets frustrating quickly. Top speed for one of these little demons was 44 miles per hour, according to the Honda service manual. When you clamp down on those 4.5-inch diameter brakes, the front end of the bike lifts up, due to the nature of the leading-link front suspension. Kind of unnerving at first, but you adjust after a while. One of the most amazing first experiences with a Honda Cub 50 is listening to it idling at a standstill—it is virtually noiseless. Many comparisons were made to an electric sewing machine of the day, and accurately so. With close-tolerance fitting of the engine components and an effective long, flat-shaped muffler, it was guaranteed not to be compared to the current crop of big-bore English and American machinery of that era. This nonoffensive behavior showed the public a different side of two-wheeled vehicles, which had been tainted by the "Wild Bunch" mentality of James Dean and the biker movies of the period.

Indicated top speed on the C100 speedometer was 40 miles per hour, but without a strong tailwind and a steep hill to ride down, that was probably an optimistic number.

Probably inspired by the female sector of the growing motorcycle population, C102 Cubs like the 1965 example, shown here, featured convenient electric-starting. *AMA*

The C110 Super Sports Cub (Sport 50) shown, in this factory photo, had the original lower sports bars. Later CA110s were changed over to higher "Western bars." C110s had all-alloy cylinder heads vs. the cast-iron versions on the C100-102-105 models. *AHMC PHOTO courtesy of John Pavich*

At various times, Honda made runs of all-chromed models as special gifts to U.S. dealers. Mostly seen as C100s like this 1962 C100T Trail 50, there were also C110s and CT200s and a few CB72/77s as well.

You could even get Y racing parts from the factory, including a racing piston, valve springs, race-kit seat, and megaphone exhaust. Don't get too excited though—a hopped-up C110 was only good for about 60–65 miles per hour.

The C110 Super Sports Cub operated like a real motorcycle, with the fuel tank between your knees, not under the seat, a clutch on the left side of the handlebars, and a manual transmission (three-speed up to 1962). The model was superseded with the CA110 Sport 50, which offered a four-speed transmission. Honda listed its top speed at 53 miles per hour, occurring at about 10,000 rpm. Not bad for an engine with a splash-fed crankshaft and transmission. Lubrication to the cylinder head was fed by a spiral groove cut in the end of the camshaft bearing; the oil was passed through a small metal tube with banjo fittings on each end and returned through a similar tube to the oil sump. A crank-mounted magneto supplied power to run the ignition, head, tail, and meter lights, as well as trickling a little juice into the 6-volt battery. Elegantly simple, easy to service, and amazingly reliable, the 50cc pushrod-engine bikes put Honda on the map worldwide.

Riding a C110 was, for many young riders, their first "normal" motorcycle riding experience after riding a C100; they had to be concerned about floating the valves only in the lower gears as they raced around at the necessary high-revs to keep out of harm's way. American hot rodders used interesting ingenuity to bore and stroke the engines out to 65cc and beyond. There were big-bore pistons, stroker crankshaft pins, racing cams, bigger carburetors, and megaphone mufflers readily available that really pushed the limits of the original design.

This standard street version of a 1961 C110 had a painted fuel tank, low handlebars, three-speed transmission, and tiny twin-bulb tail light assembly. *Bill Orazio collection*

The CY110 roadracing options included megaphone exhaust (high or low), racing seat, and special low handlebars. *Bill Orazio collection*

With the addition of the optional CY 110 Scrambler kit, the C110 was ready for off-road excursions. *Bill Orazio collection*

P50 Little Honda (1967–68)

The P50 moped, also known as the Motorwheel, is an intriguing piece of design work. The entire engine and centrifugal clutch/transmission assembly are built into the rear wheel as an integral unit. Powered by a 50cc OHC (overhead cam) two-valve engine with a compression ratio of 9:1, the rated horsepower (pony power in this case) is 1.2 at a roaring 4,200 rpm. The engine is muffled by a frying pan–sized silencer mounted just forward of the rear axle. The air filter and connecting tube to the tiny downdraft carburetor are mounted within the pressed steel frame, and the filter element is accessed through a cover on the left side beneath the seat mount. The engine cases are vertically split and the right-side case incorporates the drive system. Amazingly compact in design and execution, its main drawback is that replacement of the rear tire requires removal of the entire engine/transmission assembly.

Riding a P50

To start the engine, the driver has to engage a handlebar-mounted compression release lever, which holds the exhaust valve slightly open, and then pedal along until the magneto-fired engine (timing fixed at 30 degrees before TDC) kicks in. There is no ignition switch for this model, so the only way to secure it is to use the fork lock. One either has to balance the machine carefully on the center stand (holding the weight on the front wheel) or pedal down the driveway. Releasing the compression lever allows the engine to regain its compression and begin to operate. As the throttle

C110s like this special chrome version were the Sport Cub models, with four-speed transmissions and manual clutches. *AMA*

The PY50, also known as the "Motorwheel," this moped, produced in 1967 and 1968, combined the engine/transmission package into the rear hub/wheel assembly. A clever idea, but changing a flat or rear tire required removal of the engine assembly! The bike shown is a 1967 example. *AMA*

opens, the increasing rpm spins the centrifugal clutch hub, the shoes contact the drive hub, and off it goes.

Rear wheel braking is accomplished by a set of contracting shoes buried deep within the powerplant, acting on the outside of the clutch assembly drum. A small front SLS drum brake assists in the speed retardation process, dragging it down from a top speed of 25 miles per hour. A lever at the rear can be flipped to disengage the motor and allow the bike to be pedaled. There are three separate roller chains in the drive system of this bike. As the relationship of the engine and front pedals is fixed, a spring-loaded tensioner takes the slack out of the chain.

Weighing in at 99 pounds, the chassis features a rigid rear suspension and miniature leading-link front fork. Tires are 2.00x17 on the-front and 2.25x17 on the rear. The fuel tank is combined with the rear rack and optional grocery baskets were available, which clipped onto the front fork-mounted rack. P50s came in either scarlet red or sky blue with ivory-colored fenders. Full lighting is powered by lighting coils in the magneto. An optional battery could be mounted adjacent to the fuel tank and was fed some rectified voltage to maintain its charge. The speedometer is cable-driven from the front wheel and is mounted into a metal headlight case, which houses a dual-beam headlamp, high beam indicator, and the lighting switch.

The handlebars are a busy place, containing the throttle, front brake, rear brake, and compression release cables, as well as the high/low beam switch and horn button. A choke cable is mounted just behind the steering head.

Starting the bike on its center stand is difficult, as the weight tends to go back to the back and the rotating rear wheel wants to launch the P50 forward as the engine picks up some revolutions. It requires quite a

The smallest of machines that carried a CL (Scrambler) designation was the CL70. Like the CL90, the frame was a pressed-steel T-bone design and carried a manual clutch, 4-speed transmission, OHC powerplant package. The original 1969 version had an integral speedometer and headlight combination, which was replaced with a separate speedometer/headlight setup on the K1-K3 versions. Cosmetic changes delineated each successive model, but the mechanical features remained consistent through the 4-year production.

balancing act to prevent this. Once it is lit, the trick is to keep it running while it warms up with the choke while refraining from giving it too much throttle; otherwise, the clutch may engage and the bike could take off.. Once it is warmed up and under way, however, the quiet little machine rolls off in an orderly but unhurried fashion, until it reaches its maximum speed.

A full-sized adult outweighs the P50 by 50-70 percent, further impeding the acceleration. Handling can be considered quick, due to the short wheelbase and the small amount of mass involved. The P50 is basically a heavy-duty bicycle with a rear-mounted motor. The brakes are adequate for a machine of this type and there is always that pedal option for inclines requiring more than 1.2 horsepower to climb.

A P50 is most at home at a large swap meet or on private, paved property. They are a grand novelty, though, and practical in a limited way. In California, you can obtain a permanent moped license for about five dollars, so if you operate close to home on flat territory, then you may enjoy the experience of a Honda P50 on public roads.

P50s were replaced the following year by the PC50, which featured a motor in the middle of the frame, away from direct attachment to the rear wheel. The frames were upgraded to include a pair of rear shock absorbers, which was a substantial improvement over the "hard-tail" of the P50. PC50s were sold from 1969–70, again in small numbers. In the land of unrestricted motorcycle pleasures, the P/PC50s were a niche item, to say the least, but one worth collecting if found in complete and good condition.

As the popularity of the smaller models grew, Honda expanded the line with some 89-cc pushrod-powered machines, such as the C200 Touring 90. This is a 1965 version. *AMA*

Honda PC50 (1969–70)

Honda's great experiment with the first Little Honda, the P50, wasn't particularly well received by owners or shop mechanics due to the integral design of the motor and rear wheel. For the owners, the bike was too unbalanced with all the weight on the rear tire. For the mechanics, a usually simple tire change became a major project. The P50 was an interesting concept, but flawed as a completely useful and serviceable machine–back to the drawing boards!

The result of some considerable rethinking was the second-generation Little Honda, called the PC50. Perhaps the "C" comes from a more central location for the 49cc motor, which is pushed forward, right beneath the driver. This allows for a longer, sleeker muffler design (replacing the frying pan–shaped version on the P50), and greatly enhances the serviceability of the rear wheel. The freer-breathing engine produces 1.8 horsepower at 5,700 rpm (up from the P50's 1.2 horsepower), even after the compression was dropped to 8.5:1 from the previous 9.0:1

By 1969, the PC50 was on the bottom end of the Honda food chain in the United States, and there were few practical applications for such a machine on American roadways. In Japan and Europe, mopeds are cheap and necessary forms of transportation, bypassing many of the restrictions and expenses of a conventional motorcycle. In the vast expanse of the United States, with 65-plus mph highways

The ancestor of the long-running CT90 was the CT200, with its pushrod engine and leading-link forks. This is a 1965 example. *Troyce Walls*

The Scrambler theme started with the 1962 CL72 250-cc machine and worked its way downward to the 160 and then to the 90-cc series bikes in 1967. This 1967 CL90 retained the Scrambler concept in a downsized version of its bigger brothers. *AMA*

Honda's first venture into small-bore overhead cam single-cylinder engines came in the form of this 1965 CS65, available in black, white, and red versions. This is a 1966 S65 Sports 65. *Troyce Walls collection*

and relatively uncluttered city roads, a moped of any kind was a "fish out of water." In 1969 the top rung of the ladder was occupied by a large predator, the CB750. The PC50 never had a chance.

OHV 90cc Singles (1963-66)

After the initial appeal of the little Cub 50s had worn off, Honda needed something more upscale. Thus, the basic OHV (overhead valve) 50cc engine was redesigned and enlarged to an 89cc version, first as the C200 Touring 90 (also known as the Honda 90) delivered in September 1963, and followed by CT200 Trail 90, in May of 1964. The

The 1970 CT90K2 introduced the swivel-lock handlebar system to aid in convenient loading and storing of Trail 90s on the back of motorhomes.

Honda 90 moniker was later reapplied to the OHC CM91 step-through model released in February 1966, so don't get those two confused. The C200 and CT200 looked like their 50cc counterparts bulked up on steroids, and they offered a little more carrying capacity and speed, but were ultimately only a temporary fix until the new OHC models came out in October 1964.

OHC 90cc Singles (1964–69)

Mr. Honda quickly realized that the potential of the U.S. market rivaled anything he had done so far. In a country without restrictions on engine displacement or licensing, the wide-open spaces of the United States would require machinery of a much larger scale. The pushrod OHV 50cc Honda Cubs and OHV 90cc models gave way to a new OHC engine series, beginning with the S65–a cute bike, which was plagued with transmission flaws–in April 1965. That was just the beginning of the upward spiral in engineering prowess and ever-improving models.

The penultimate year of CT90 production was 1978, before Honda enlarged the engine to create the CT110 in 1980. Final CT110s were produced in 1986, after a full 20-year run! *AMA*

Unchanged from 1984 to 86, the CT110 Trail 110 was the last of the hardy Trail machines that began back in the early 1960s. Except for the initial 1980 version, most CT110 models featured dual range transmissions, and 1982–1986 models featured CDI ignitions. *Terry Brigham*

Honda responded to the need for speed in the step-through series with the CM91, an 89-cc overhead cam version produced from 1966 until 1969. In 1970, it went back the other way with the release of the 1970–1973 C70 Honda 70 (and later 1980–1983 C70 Passport) series. *AMA*

The new OHC S90 (Super 90) came forward in October 1964, joined by the OHC CT90KO Trail 90 in April 1966 and the CL90 Scrambler in March 1967. The S90 and CL90s are closely related fundamentally and differ only in cosmetic details. Tough and reliable, they thrived in the hands of young riders, who had "graduated" from the 50s.

The basic OHC S90 engine, fitted with a dual-range transmission and automatic clutch, was transplanted into the pushrod CT200 Trail 90 step-through frame and became the new CT90 Trail 90, which endured from 1966 to 1979 and was then bumped up to 110ccs as a Trail 110. CT90s had leading-link suspension until 1969, when telescopic forks were fitted. When the swivel-lock handlebar-mounting system was introduced in 1970, these bikes were plastered all over the backs of motor homes as a local transportation piece for those who preferred not to trailer along an extra car. They have become sought-after collectibles today.

S90 & CL90 Scramblers (1964–69)

These fine, rugged, OHC horizontal singles were offered as the next generation replacements to the short-lived C200/CT200 pushrod singles of 1963–64. The S90 was released in late 1964, as a sleek little brother to the CB160-series twins. These bikes were based on a strong but simple T-bone-shaped pressed-steel frame, with

The Rally Kit from the Honda Custom Group enabled would-be racers to at least look as if they were fulfilling track fantasies by dressing up pedestrian CM91s with racy bodywork. *AMA*

a separate rear fender and telescopic forks, as an evolution of the previous heavy Benly-style frames with integral rear fender sections and leading-link front suspension.

While the C200 is rated at 6.5 horsepower, the new S90 pumps out 8. At only 175 pounds, the S90 can achieve speeds over 65 miles per hour, and can often see 70 if the driver tucks down out of the wind.

Light and nimble, they were the first "real motorcycle" for many 1960s baby boomers and were subject to any number of modifications, including big-bore kits, racing cams, special manifolds (mounting CB72 or CB77 carburetors), and so on. S90s were turned into roadracers, trail bikes, TT machines, and just about anything else you might imagine.

First generation S90s have kind of a twisted intake manifold. This intake arrangement requires a specifically designed air cleaner system to adapt the carburetor to the machine. The next series wears a simple straight-back curved intake manifold with a Keihin carburetor and a revised air filter and housing. If you are restoring any OHC 90 engine, take note of the arrangement of the intake manifold–mounting flange pattern on the cylinder head. There are two different patterns: straight across and angled. Because so many of the heads look the same, you have to be certain that you are matching the part you are

Released in 1965 as a replacement for the pushrod C200 street machine, the new S90s had a simple-but-effective overhead-valve engine design and a new conventional telescopic fork in place of the previous leading-link fork design. S90s were the hit of the day for many young riders, stepping up from the 50cc machines. A healthy S90 will approach 70 miles per hour. *AMA*

Early versions of S90 machines sported painted fenders, lower handlebars, and convoluted intake manifolds, but lacked turn signals, in comparison with the 1968 and later models. *Bret Samms collection*

replacing, otherwise you will be forced to go manifold and air cleaner shopping, and your whole restoration will be incorrect.

There are several different muffler mounting systems, so this is another area to watch when selecting a replacement part. A number of internal engine modifications were affected over the years, so you must be careful not to wind up with a bucket full of S90, ST90, CT90, and ATC90 parts during your parts searches, of which any number may not fit or function properly in an S90 application.

The CL90 Scramblers were brought into the United States for the 1968 model season, and they were sharp little imitations of their bigger brothers, the CL160 and the CL72/77s. They were based on the S90, but the CL90s had a different seat, tank, fenders, handlebars, and exhaust pipe.

The 1974 CB125S1, a 122-cc street machine, was packed with features for a bike of its size. The front drum brake of the previous year's model was replaced with a self-adjusting cable-operated disc brake, downsized from a similar version on the CB200T. So effective was the brake that it was grafted onto the front of the 1977 MT125R two-stroke road racer, which had a top speed of 110 miles per hour! Other amenities included a center stand, speedometer AND tachometer, 18-inch front and 17-inch rear wheels, and a full set of turn signals. Top speed was 65 miles per hour. *AMA*

Both S90 and CL90s are mechanically similar and have full-sized 18-inch wheels, whereas their predecessors have only 17-inch hoops. This makes replacement tire selection a little easier and makes the bike feel more substantial underneath the driver when cornering or having a go at the rough stuff. The S/CL90s are very quiet, well-muffled, and user-friendly. While the pushrod engines are all done at about 8,500 rpm, the OHC versions are seemingly unbreakable, running at 9,500 rpm and beyond. In the late 1970s, in ATC applications, these engines were bored and stroked to 180ccs and ran on alcohol, probably making over 25 horsepower.

Restoring S90 and CL90s is a typical Honda adventure, for although the basic chassis and engine configurations are the same, the external bodywork is all different, and even the tank badges are distinctly different. The S90 tank badges are marked "S90," whereas the CL90 badges show only the number "90" below the wing.

CB/CL/SL100-125s (1970–75)

Honda made millions of OHC 90 engines for many applications, but they were stretched as far as they could go at 110cc, and cooling was somewhat restricted, due to the horizontal cylinder placement directly behind the front wheel and fender. In 1970, Honda replaced the design with the nearly vertical CB100 engine (CB90 in Japan), which featured a new five-speed transmission. This engine was easily bored out by Honda to 122cc, and became the CB/CL125 (also a short-lived CT125) street bikes. Both engines saw service in Motosport chassis as SL100 and SL125 machines. The SL125 became an XL125 in 1974; was given a six-speed transmission and bumped up to a 185cc displacement becoming the XL185S in 1979; then stretched again in 1980 to 195cc for TLR/XL/XR200 duty, doubling the original displacement!

The Honda CB125s of 1974–78 features a unique, cable-operated front disc brake, which was also adapted to the first version of the MT125R road racers. The original CB100/125 cylinder head is a single-piece and somewhat prone to wearing its camshaft-bearing surfaces. In 1976 the engine was revamped with a new two-piece head, revised valve angles and sizes, and an intake port divider, which was designed to maintain high port velocity at midthrottle settings. The 1976 125 engines were also bumped up to 124cc, with a small increase in bore size. In 1981 the points-type ignition was replaced by a CDI. The 1984–85 Brazilian-made models were upgraded to a 12v system. CL100/125s pretty much followed the CB-series machines but always had a small drum brake on the front wheel and, of course, wore those high-mounted Scrambler exhaust pipes.

FT500 (1982–83)

Apart from the retro-look 1989–90 GB500 singles, the only other large-displacement street single Honda has offered os the FT500 Ascot single, based on the XL/XR500 dirt bike engine/chassis and equipped with large front disc brake and cast wheels on both ends—an interesting interim step used to fill in the 500cc range of street bikes in 1982–83. Ultimately, it was a niche-market bike that couldn't find its niche. FT500s were offered for only two years (1982–83) and faced a lot of competition from other models in the lineup (VT500 Ascot, for one), as well as from other makers during that era.

FT500s vary from their dirt-oriented brethren by their shortened travel in the suspension, as well as small variations to the engine cases and covers, which facilitate a tach drive and a 12-volt charging system. The engine size and cylinder head have the same configuration as the XL/XR bikes, with a 35-millimeter carburetor mounted on the single inlet port and exhaust gases exiting the dual exhaust ports. The 2:1 down pipes feeds a single, left-side–mounted muffler, coated in shiny black paint.

The 1982 models suffered from defective electric starter drive problems, though, so be wary of those early versions. There is no kick starter option for this model, so a healthy electrical system is vital to keep this bike on the road.

Finding original, low-mileage editions of these bikes is getting increasingly difficult because they were only produced for two years, and they are certainly considered collectibles by 1980s enthusiasts. The only difference between the 1982 and 1983 versions were the electric starter update, minor graphics changes, and the replacement of the 1982 85 miles per hour speedometer with a 120 miles per hour unit in 1983. Two colors were offered, red and black, with matching graphics.

The FT500s are still actively raced in Thumper classes of vintage racing organizations and can be modified with many of the same parts as the XL/XR models. Big-bore pistons, high-performance cams/valves, bigger carburetors, and a suitable racing exhaust can coax as much as 60 horsepower from these engines. The front forks are a little on the slender side, and racers have found that the larger front forks from a Hawk GT650 are a direct bolt-on, greatly improving the handling and stability at racing speeds.

1950s British thumper styling, combined an electric-start, counter-balanced 500-cc, four-valve single with modern disc brake stopping, to create the 1989-90 GB500. *Terry Brigham collection*

Is it a single or a twin? Note the dual exhaust pipes from dual-port head feeding into a single muffler. *Terry Brigham collection*

GB500 (1989–90)

GB500s were also a two-year machine, crippled by a $4,200 initial price in 1989, lowered $500 the following year. Finally, in desperation, they were blown out of dealerships at $2,900 a couple of years later. Based loosely on the RVFC four-valve XL500 engine, these beauties were fashioned in the likeness of the late 1950s–early 1960s British Thumpers, like the Norton Manx, BSA Oldster, and Velocity. GB500s have lovely, heavy-duty, wire spoke wheels and a disc brake on the front. Low clip-on bars completed the effect of a British-style cafe racer.

With the rise in bike prices since their 1989 introduction, they would be a steal if offered again for the same money and with just a little more horsepower. Still, they will fetch mid-$2,000 to mid-$3,000 and up prices, if in mint original condition.

If ever there was a love-hate relationship with a motorcycle, the GB500 pushed all of the passion buttons simultaneously. Lovely to behold and crafted with typical Honda thoughtfulness, the arrival of the GB500 was applauded for its beautiful retro-style shapes and then booed for its lackluster performance and astounding price of $4,195. Aside from the modern hydraulic front disc brake and a few plastic bits, Honda had captured all of the styling essence of the 1950s British singles and combined it with modern easy electric-starting and a counterbalanced, four-valve (RFVC) dry-sump engine that kept all of its oil inside the motor. While the 250/400s had seating for two, the U.S.-market GB500 had only a solo seat and lacked a centerstand for easy maintenance, something offered in other countries' versions of the machine.

Honda's only two-stroke street bike in the United States was the 1982 MB-5, a screaming 10,500-rpm 50-cc minirocket! Packed with features such as CDI ignition, counterbalanced engine, five-speed transmission, mag wheels, front disc brake, and full street lighting, they hit the market at $895, ready to go and available in red or black. After one year of limited sales, they were another footnote in Honda's history book. In Europe, they were available as an MB-8, with 80 cc to propel them down the road.

The GB500 motor was based on the XL500 dual-purpose engine and was muffled down substantially, then had an external pulse-air smog system grafted onto the outside of the engine. The EPA standards mandated carbon canisters and jetting was on the lean side for low emissions. Rated at 40 crankshaft horsepower at 7,000 rpm in Japan, they were obviously not putting out that kind of power in the U.S. (about 33 rear wheel horsepower on the U.S. dynos). With 390 pounds of machine to haul around, the overall effect was smooth and torquey but not awe-inspiring. Certainly, with the wealth of performance-tuning resources available in the United States for the XL/XR500/600s, the power could be found in the basic design, but at a substantial extra cost.

The GB500s sat in dealers' showrooms for several years after they were first released, the sticker prices holding off prospective suitors. The price was reduced $500 for the 1990 models, but that still wasn't sufficient to woo new buyers. Honda finally chose to dump the remaining stock at fire-sale prices and you could waltz one out the door for less than $3,000 at the end. GB500s seemed to have wound up either as minor-league collectors items, if kept in pristine condition, or they went the way of the "I like mine hot" league and got the bolt-on 600cc top end, a healthy dose of camshaft, big carburetor, and a lightweight exhaust with a big bass sound. The hopped-up ones usually shed their air pumps and bulky air boxes and get some stronger fork springs and performance rear shocks to help keep some sticky compound tires carving through twisty turns.

The standard GB500 truly is a beautiful thing to behold and will catch the attention of anyone remotely interested in motorcycles. As mentioned, the noise level sounds more like a stationary generator than "500cc of Thumper Power," in the standard trim. The clip-on bars, mounted above the upper triple clamp, are not too low for most riders, but the combination of weight load and angularity can cause a little wrist discomfort in a short while, especially around town. You will become quickly accustomed to the machine, especially if you are a Honda rider by habit. Controls are light and the instruments are easy to see, except on a sunny day when the silver-faced instruments can wash out.

Honda sought to keep the refined ride of a typical Honda street bike product and fitted soft springs in the front forks. The rear dampers were, as usual, under-damped, although adjustable for preload. Riding the bike on a freeway is deceiving, due to the low level of vibration and noise. There is no discernible bump in the power curve; just a flat band of torque and smooth increase in the rate of travel when the throttle is opened up. There is little vibration or noise at 70 mph—quite amazing for a 500cc "Thumper." For those used to winding the tachometer into the five-digits zone, there is little thrill in taking the GB500 to redline. "Competent, but a little boring," is the usual reaction of those who have taken a stock bike for a short ride.

Such is the paradox of riding and/or owning a GB500. Many are stored in garages, just so that they can be appreciated for their beauty and execution of design. Serious riders, however, are seldom able to withstand the temptation of doing some basic modifications to the intake and exhaust systems in order to bring the machine up to a higher level of performance and to fully appreciate the design.

Chapter 3

The 125-250cc Twins (1959–87)

Honda built 90cc to 350cc single-cylinder bikes exclusively until 1957, when the first of its dry-sump 250-305cc twins began to appear. Mr. Honda's passion for high-performance engines was based on his belief that the more revolutions an engine could turn, the more power it could make. While some of the OHC singles would turn up to 7,500 rpm, rider comfort suffered from the vibrations, so smaller twin-cylinder engines were an obvious answer to a reduction of vibration as well as an increase of rider comfort and overall performance.

Honda's first twin, the 1957 250cc C70 Dream makes four more horsepower than the earlier ME single and still weighs 40 pounds less overall. Honda took the same concept to the smaller displacement machines and created the 125cc C92 Benly, which makes 11.5 horsepower at an amazing 9,500 rpm. Digging deeper into the concept of lightweight and high-revving performance for sporting enthusiasts yielded the 1959 CB92 (briefly available as a 150cc version CB95), which makes 15 horsepower from its tiny twin motor that breathes through a single, 18-millimeter carburetor.

CB92 and CA/95 Twins Overview

Once the beachhead was established with the Honda Cubs, Honda began to introduce the bigger machines. The 1960 Honda 125cc CB92 Super Sport and 150cc CA95 Benly were rolled as alternatives to the beginner bikes and they were real eye-openers for novice and experienced enthusiasts alike. The CB92 features alloy fuel tank, side covers, front fender, and 8-inch magnesium DLS brakes on the front wheel. An angular fuel tank features a wraparound knee pad, and the short, flat handlebars give an immediate impression of power and style. Honda claimed that a stock CB92 would go 81 miles per hour and about 85 miles per hour for the race-kitted version. The YB (accessory) parts

"Honda Wins Again!" This ad, from an early motorcycle publication, proclaimed the successes of the new CB92 in competition, both in the dirt and on paved racing tracks.

list included a racing-style seat, 13,000 rpm tachometer, megaphone exhausts, and numerous racing-spec engine parts, allowing the power curve to reach over 10,500 rpm. This kind of performance from a street-based production motorcycle was unheard of in 1960. Even the "convenient" CA95 Benly sister machine would reach 70 miles per hour; and both had single-carburetor two-valve cylinder heads, electric-starting, oil-tight engines, and amazingly detailed fittings on each machine. The really astounding part was the fact that Honda could mass-produce these bikes by the thousands every day!

Benly 125 Super Sport (1959–64)

CB92s (Benly 125s) and a one-year only CB95 (the 150cc version) were sold first in Japan in 1959. These machines were even used as practice bikes for the first Isle of Man races attended by Honda factory riders. The bikes are powered by a wet-sump OHC, two valves per cylinder, 360 degree firing, and a parallel twin engine producing 15 horsepower at 10,500 rpm. The camshaft is driven by a chain from the left end of the crankshaft. The transmission is a four-speed unit, with wet-clutch and electric-starting. Front suspension was a leading-link design and wheels were 18-inch front and rear, with spokes laced to magnesium 8-inch hubs and fitted with DLS brakes on the front and SLS on the rear. The large-capacity 6-volt batteries are charged by a permanent-magnet generator, which was driven off the left end of the crankshaft.

The 1960 bikes have "Benly" tank badges rather than the "Benly 125" shown on the later versions. The first bikes have alloy tanks, side covers, and front fenders. The original cables are of smaller diameter and the levers have small-balled tips. The tool kits are quite complete and include the tire pump lock keys, scissors, and a tire patch kit. The lockable tire pump is located below the fuel tank in special welded-on brackets.

Service and overhaul is pretty much standard Honda, if you have been working on many of the era's models. It helps to have watch-maker genes in your DNA makeup, as everything is on the small side when you begin overhauling the engines and making carburetor changes. These bikes aren't particularly complicated, but they do have an orderly and definite sequence in which to do maintenance or repair operations.

CB92s were available as street-legal street bikes or as "YB race-kit" racers, known as a CB92R model. A long list of YB parts was available over the counter to convert a street machine to race-kit specs, as well. These engines were capable of 12,000 rpm in race trim and speeds approaching 90 miles per hour. *AMA*

In Japanese, "Benly" means convenient. *Bill Orazio*

This close-up of the 1959 C95 engine shows a distributor cap ignition system that was nicknamed the "dust cap." *Bill Orazio*

The suspension is very taut and you are continually bounced around on either the dual or the YB racing seat. The 8-inch brakes are overkill on a 275-pound bike like this, and application of the front brakes causes the leading link suspension to rise up.

If you happen to be CB92 shopping, be prepared–there were three different crankshaft designs used in the first three years of the machines. Numerous other detail items were modified or changed according to U.S. safety standards. Apparently, the non-U.S. windscreens were not on the approved list, as the part numbers for the screens and attaching hardware were deleted on subsequent parts lists after 1964. There were four different taillight assemblies, four different fuel tanks, and a couple of transmission changes, and the original alloy body parts were superseded by steel replacements through the years. Many CB92s were improved with the adaptation of CA95 150cc top ends. The original 124cc cylinders, cylinder heads, and 18-millimeter carburetors were tossed, making restoration-to-original specs projects almost impossible. There were many crankshaft failures in the first two years and oftentimes, a whole CA95 motor was transplanted into the chassis. Be aware that both engine side covers and kickstart/shifter shafts are narrower than the 150cc Benly counterparts.

There is a series of C92 125cc Benlys which have low-compression pistons and a crankshaft that is not supported between the crank throws. Sometimes these bottom ends (or whole engines) are employed to revive a CB92 chassis. The engine cases will be stamped C92 and not CB92, so look carefully. Some CA95 cases have had their numbers modified, in an attempt to match the chassis numbers. Generally, the engine and chassis numbers are within 150 numbers of each other.

Serial numbers

1960 CB92-60-00001 or CB92-00001 frame;
    CB92E-0100001 engine
1961 CB92-100001 frame; CB92E-110001 engine
1962 CB92-200001 frame; CB92E-2100001 engine
1963 CB92-300001 frame; CB92E-3100001 engine
1964 CB92-700001 frame; CB92E-7100001 engine

Note: Frame numbers are generally found on the left side of the frame at the rear just behind the left side covers, if not seen on the left side of the steering head. Whole books could be written about the minutiae of these machines. In all, some 24,000 units were produced from 1959 to 1964, but after only 51 reported sales of 1962 street versions, the model was terminated in the United States. Despite this, production continued and bikes were sold in Europe, the UK, and Japan through 1964. Those bikes generally have 300001 and 700001 serial numbers for the 1963–64 models.

As these bikes often trade hands for anywhere from $1,000 to over $7,500, one really has to be astute to prevent from getting burned by an incorrect or unoriginal "restoration" of these unique models. Do be careful here–check serial numbers at the very least, and try to contact those who have restored the bikes in the past to verify correct features pertaining to each year's model. Getting a copy of the Honda parts manual will be of great assistance in this case. It is probably too late in the game to begin a restoration of a CB92, unless it is very complete and in generally good condition to begin with. The CB92s are definite conversation pieces and worth having if your goal is to own a unique and classic Honda model.

As a final warning, a few CA95 chassis have been modified to accept CB92 forks, fuel tanks, seats, and so on, and passed off as CB92s. A famous fake was shown in the 1974 Phil Schilling book *The Motorcycle World,* unbeknownst to the author. It was later discovered to be a 1962 CA95 with a CB92 front end, mufflers, wheels, and bodywork!

Return of the 125 Twin: SS125 Super Sport & CL125 Scrambler (1967–69)

In late 1967, Honda returned a pair of 125cc street twins to the market in the form of the SS125 and CL125, both based on the CD125 model sold elsewhere. Looking at the parts manual, one would think that Honda had revived the tooling for the CB92s again, as the design of the engine is very similar. Both engines share the similar left-side chain-driven camshafts, four-speed gearboxes, and single-carburetor cylinder heads. The carburetor was now a CV-style, with a rubber diaphragm controlled slide; and although the engine internals look the same, virtually all of the part numbers are different. The frame is a T-bone stamped steel unit, similar to the S90. There was a nice tube-framed, dual-carburetor version available outside the United States, but it was never released here.

The SS model has a longish, racy-looking silver fuel tank and slight riser handlebars, giving it quite a sporty effect, while the CL125 Scramblers feature the "Baby CL77" look with cross-braced bars, rounded fuel tank, abbreviated fenders, different patterned seats, and large "125" plastic tank emblems with accompanying rubber kneepads. The CL125 and CL160 are so similar in style that one could confuse the two from 20 feet

Honda seemed to think that there was still a gap to be filled between the S90 and the CB160, so it inserted the SS125 twin into the line-up. The basic engine design mimicked the earlier CB92 in many ways, but no parts are interchangeable. Still breathing through a single diaphragm-controlled carburetor, its speed was restricted to about 65 miles per hour. A companion CL125 model was sold alongside the SS to complete the Street/Scrambler duet at each level. *AMA*

Available in black, white, red, and blue (with a blue seat cover), the CB160 filled an important gap between the little street singles and the larger 250–305-cc lineup of bikes. *Troyce Walls collection*

away. Performance-wise, they are both very tame and sales were not up to expectations. Honda was bumping heads with leftover CB/CL160s as well as the new 175s, and the bikes were quietly dropped in 1969.

CB160 Super Sport & CL160 Scrambler (1964–69)

In mid-1964, Honda finally filled in the gap left by the CB92s in the small-bore street bike category. CA95s were the only small-twin option available between 1962 and the release of the 160s in 1964. The newly designed machines were little jewels, crafted in the likeness of their CB/CL77 big brothers. The cam chains now ran down the center of the two cylinders, and dual 20-millimeter carburetors were fitted to the dual-port cylinder heads. Electric starters grace the CBs but were deleted on the CLs until a run of CL160D models with electric starters was

Placed midway between the S90 and the CB72, the CB160 targeted buyers upgrading from the little singles. Styled as a 7/8th scale CB72, the CB and CL160s were sharp-handling, fun-to-ride lightweight twins. *AMA*

released in mid-1967. The original CL160s are black, framed with a silver tank, side covers, and fork legs, whereas the CL160Ds are available in the standard quartet of black/scarlet, red/blue, and white, just like the CB160s had been all along. There were also D-kit scramblers, created by installing a Scrambler conversion kit on a CB160. These kits featured metallic orange or blue fuel tanks, similar to the early CL175s. The standard CB160D bikes have color-matched fuel tanks and frames. Over the years, I have heard about dealerships having dozens of CB160 mufflers, tanks, seats, and handlebars in stock, due to the large number of D conversion kits that they used to supply the demand of Scrambler-styled bikes.

Honda's CB160s were cherished by young riders who couldn't afford the CB77s or whose parents wouldn't let them ride a "big" motorcycle. Equipped with full-sized 18-inch wheels, the bikes were a joy to ride and the 7-inch DLS brakes are just as powerful on these lightweights as the 8-inch binders on the bigger bikes. The 160s were sturdily built in typical Honda fashion, and a little heavy at 279 pounds. With the standard four-speed transmissions, the only way to get the most out of the machine is to ride it wide open all the time. Rated at 16.5 horsepower at 10,000 rpm, they were just freeway-legal, at least in California. They were hot sellers just about everywhere in the U.S. The little CL160s were often found running in the tracks of the CL77s, out in the back-country hills and fire roads, owing their popularity to their relationship to the hot-selling, full-sized Scramblers. This is a fine series of machines, having excellent handling and braking characteristics in addition to their very stylish looks.

Honda shapes the world of wheels

The unusual blue/blue seat combination on this 1967 CB160 was yet another way that Honda shaped the world of two-wheeled transportation, as this centerfold magazine ad claims. *AHMC*

America was wild for Scramblers, and the Honda CL160 was another opportunity for beginning riders to experience the CL-series machines. Honda even sold kits to convert standard CB160s into CL160s. *AMA*

Benlys: CA95/CA160/CA175/CD175 (1959-70)

The CA95 Benly Touring 150 was a big-bore version of the domestic 124-cc CA92, and was designed as a short-haul machine for local errands or trips to school. This particular machine was painted *pink* from the factory! *Troyce Walls*

From 1959, the Benly series 150-160-175cc bikes ran a parallel path with the Super Sport and Scrambler bikes, evolving from the side-cam–driven 150cc engines to the central-driven 160s, then a short-lived "slant-engine" 160-based CL175, before their final incarnation as a nearly vertical 175. All the machines from this series (except the CA175s) have four-speed, single-carburetor engines and feature similar angular fenders, sheet-metal frames, enclosed drive-chains, and the same, poorly damped leading-link front suspension with 16-inch wheels. The CA160/175s became Touring 160-175 models instead of Benlys. Introduced in the spring of 1968, the CA175 features telescopic forks and round shocks, headlights, and fenders but still retains the pressed-steel frame construction.

While useful and popular as basic transportation in Japan and Europe, the lack of power, lackluster suspension, and awkward styling left a lot to be desired as far as the U.S. market was concerned. Thus, the sales numbers suffered and the bikes never got a great deal of attention in the States. Restorers often find many parts available for these machines due to the lack of enthusiasm for repairing them in the 1960s.

The final incarnation of the Benly-designed machines was the CA175. Earlier editions featured the "sloper" designed engine, which was replaced with the more modern "vertical" configuration. The whole Benly/Touring 160-175 series was never fully embraced in the United States, due to lack of restrictions here that were imposed in European and Asian markets.

The CB175K4 was a classy look-alike for the CB/CL350 machines. *Honda photo courtesy of Bill Orazio*

CB/CL/CM/SL175/185/200/250s (1968–83)

In 1967 the CA/CB/CL160 series machines were finally upgraded to 175cc and (except for the CD/CA175s) given a five-speed transmission as well. Oddly, no CB175 was offered for one year in the United States, only the CL175. Perhaps this was due to the popularity of the Scrambler-style bikes. In 1969 the 175s followed the tradition of the CB160s (looking like their bigger brothers, the CB/CL77), and became junior versions of the larger CB350s both in style and in engine configuration. The cylinders were also raised to near vertical from the previous forward-sloped position. The new 175 machines were joined by their Motosport brother, the SL175, in 1970. The SL175 ran only until 1972, but CB/CL sales continued until 1973. Like their predecessors, the 175s always have a solid feel to them. Honda put strength in any area where there might be a problem, so they might be heavy, but they are never flimsy in either materials or execution of design. The 175s were great for new riders and ladies who might feel intimidated by the heft of a 350. They offer a firm, controlled ride, excellent brakes, and quiet, reliable, economical performance.

Electric starters, DLS front brakes, and five-speed transmissions of the CL175K4 made for safe, quiet performance and easy operation. *Honda photo courtesy of Bill Orazio*

Honda superseded the CB/CL175 series with a pair of CB/CL200 twins. The CB200 features a front cable-operated disc brake. *Bill Orazio*

CB/CL200 (1974–76)

The 1974–76 CB/CL200s were the replacements for the CB/CL/SL 175 machines. The CB200 has a novel cable-operated front disc brake, while the CL has to make do with the usual DLS drum stopper up front. The CS/CL200S is an enlarged version of the CB/CL175 engine series, but with upgrades like larger wrist pins and similar strengthening.

CM185-200-250 (1978–82)

After a one-year pause in the small-bike product line, the new CM-series Twinstar minicustoms were released from 1978 to 1980 as 185cc versions, then in 200cc sizes for 1980 to 1982. Honda introduced a restyled CM250C with a new five-speed transmission in 1982 and then added a toothed-belt on the final drive for 1983. These bikes are low-powered, single-carburetor twins that work well for shorter or more cautious beginning riders.

The 200-cc engines used in the CB/CL200 bikes, which are enlarged versions of the original 160-cc engines, were upgraded with larger wrist pins and rubber-mounted carbs. *Bill Orazio*

CMX250 Rebel (1985–87)

In 1985, a serious redo of the little CM250 twins into junior-sized Cruisers–called the Honda 250 Rebels–suddenly sparked a huge interest in these baby choppers, and the dealers were swamped with orders. The Rebel was one of Honda's top-selling bikes that year. There was even a Limited edition with gold trim and pseudo-flamed decals on the tank. Performance-wise, Rebels are pretty much all done after 80 miles per hour, but the little disc brake, fitted on the front of such a light machine, gives some of the shortest stopping distances ever recorded at one of the motorcycle magazine's test beds.

Essentially a bored-out version of the CM185 Twinstar, the CM200, with its single carb and four-speed transmission, was low-maintenance and low-performance. *AMA*

Chopperesque looks and a catchy ad campaign contributed more to the success of Honda's CMX250C Rebel than the performance of the motorcycle itself.

The Classic 250–350cc Twins (1960–67)

The first 250cc machines, brought to the United States during the 1958–60 period, were dry-sump (separate oil tanks) versions of the basic Dream model (sheet-metal frames, single carburetor, leading-link front suspension, and 16-inch wheels). Honda was busy creating a new line of bikes for the 1961 model year, and when these were previewed at the International Motorcycle shows, even the hard-core motorcyclists of the time were stunned. The new, wet-sump versions of the Dream were accompanied by the new 250cc CB72 Hawk and 305cc CB77 Super Hawk (Super Sports) models, featuring tubular frames, telescopic front forks, and 18-inch front and rear wheels with 8-inch DLS brakes on both ends. The bikes are equipped with electric-starting and the new sports models have twin carburetors of either 22 or 26 millimeters, which are huge compared to those of similar bikes of the era.

This 1960 CA71 Dream Touring 250 awaits restoration and some correct mufflers as well. This year marked the end of the dry-sump models and the beginning of the newly designed wet-sump C72-77 machines. *Bill Orazio collection*

MEET THE RECORD-BREAKING HONDA SUPER HAWK!

THERE'S NEVER BEEN ANYTHING LIKE IT ANYWHERE — AT ANY TIME — AT ANY PRICE!

The SUPER HAWK is the proudest creation from HONDA'S great stable of champions... the unbeatable machines that have swept the Isle of Man and every other international Grand Prix classic.

We could list the SUPER HAWK's specifications—but they tell only half the story. For HONDA design and engineering is such that performance begins where specifications leave off.

Once you've tested the might of a SUPER HAWK, you'll know why HONDA is the choice of experts... and why it will be your choice, too!

It's here—ready—and rarin' to go! Why not try it today?

World's Largest Motorcycle Manufacturer

Full Price ONLY $ ....

This rare sales flyer shows the ground-breaking 1961 CB72 Sports 250-cc Sports machines from Honda.

Hawks, Super Hawks, Scramblers, and Dreams (1960–67)

Hawks, Scramblers, and Dreams all share the same basic chassis, with slightly different equipment. The CB72 Hawk and CB77 Superhawk are more sporting-oriented streetbikes, the CA72 and CA77 Dreams are simple street bikes, and the CL72 and CL77 Scramblers are off-road-capable machines.

CB72-77

Until 1966, these bikes had color-matched Type 1 frames and forks in the United States. The final 1966–67 versions have alloy fork legs that were painted silver. 1965 was a transitional year for both flat bars and the "reverse-needle" (needles face opposite directions and move from bottom to top) speedo/tachometers, which were replaced with higher western bars and the concentric meters (both needles go the same direction) on the CB72-77.

CL72-77

Special note should be made of the CL72-77 250-305cc Scramblers (released in 1962), which opened up a new category of bikes for Japanese motorcycle enthusiasts. Although the engines are closely aligned with those of the CB72/77, they are otherwise completely different. For openers, the shedding of the electric starters lightened up the motors and reduced some low-slung, unsprung weight. The frame is a closed loop, with a down tube for rigidity and strength. The CL72s made their mark by successfully navigating a Baja Mexico adventure way before there were many organized races or decent roads. Honda was justly proud of this accomplishment and advertised it heavily to introduce the new model. The compact fuel tank, slender alloy fenders, and distinctive sound of the stylish high-mounted exhaust pipes burned the images of Scramblers in the minds of Honda fans for years. The Super Hawks and Scrambler s are considered to be some of the most desirable models of the 1960s.

This photo shows an original, 1961 CB77 in mint condition with the early single leading shoe front brake.
Pat Jones

Wet-sump Dreams like the 1963 version shown here were available from 1961 to 1967. Engines were related to the CB/CL77 models, but had lower compression and single carburetors. *AMA*

Honda's brilliant sports machine, the CB77 Super Hawk 305, featured electric-starting, an oil-tight engine, 28 horsepower, and a 100-mile per hour top speed. *Bill Orazio collection*

CA72/77s

These are distinctly different in styling (mostly with the fuel tanks) in the 1961–62 versions versus the late-1962 and onwards models. There were changes in the battery boxes and swingarm/chain guards in 1965. These parts will not interchange with earlier bikes.

CB72 Hawks and CB77 Super Hawks (1961–67)

The 250cc Hawk and 305cc Super Hawk has redlines of 9,500 rpm, and Honda claimed that the 305 version is capable of 100 miles per hour. Honda released an extensive list of bolt-on, high-performance parts. Someone who bought the entire kit could literally build a race-ready machine in a few hours.

Compared to competitive bikes of the day, the CB77 Super Hawk handled well, had decent power, and was quite smooth. Compared to a halfway-decent 1970s multicylinder, the Super Hawk is

The 1966 CB77 Super Hawk featured new alloy fork sliders with external fork springs, although you couldn't see them with the fork covers in place. Mechanically, they were pretty similar to the original 1961 versions, with a host of small modifications to correct problems that cropped up over the years. The CB77 would have one more year of production before being replaced by the new five-speed CB350 in 1968. *AMA*

slow and buzzy. However, considering that a 400-pound, four-cylinder, four-carburetor 1975 CB400F has a top speed of maybe 105 miles per hour, the CB77 can't be considered a slug. Most stock Super Hawks in a top state of tune would break 100 miles per hour.

The stock bike looks just right with the original, early-style, flat handlebars. The rear shocks are sturdy but have little damping, so it is best to replace them with aftermarket items that help the rear end stay planted. The front forks are pretty weak on damping too, but will keep

This 1966 CB77 features some CBY parts, such as rear-set footpegs, rear number plate bracket, alloy YB rims, YB seat, and a CB92 taillight assembly on alloy YB rear fender. *Bill Silver*

With its fork cover removed, the external springs used in the 1966 CB77 are clearly visible. *Bill Silver*

you out of trouble. For most average-sized riders, the bike fits just fine. The seats are pretty comfortable for an hour or so, if the foam hasn't collapsed yet (which is unlikely these days).

Properly adjusted and bedded-in, the DLS front and rear brakes are reasonable, but they are still drum brakes. Unfortunately, because of the DLS configuration, they don't work well if you are holding the bike facing uphill. The engineering focus at that time was on stopping the bike going forward, not backward.

Super Hawks are safe and steady at high speeds, and economical too. Fuel mileage seldom dips below 50 miles per gallon, no matter how hard they are ridden. All of the available power seems to be applied to moving the machine forward, as the internal collection of ball, needle, and roller bearings reduces internal friction to an absolute minimum. Oil fed to the engine internals comes from a splash feed and drip system, just enough to keep everything wet. An oil pressure gauge would show just about zero all of the time! Considering that a great deal of the design was formulated in the late 1950s, Super Hawks are truly a remarkable piece of engineering.

Many people think that the CB77 is the most collectible model, due to its sleek styling and reasonable performance (for a 305cc bike). The electric starter is just the thing to keep the bruises off of your shins. You will understand if you try to kick-start this model, which is equipped with a forward-kicking starter arm. This feature fascinates people to no end, but it just about always whacks you in the shins when you are forced to use it. If your electric starter is inoperative, it is better to bump-start it than to kick it. This brings up another point: the forward motion starter came about with the addition of an intermediate gear in the kick-starter cover. This whole design weakened the integrity of the cover and CB72–77s are often found with their kick-starter covers cracked or broken in two.

The tires are narrow at 2.75x18 on the front and 3.00x18 on the rear, making it easy to lock up the rear wheel with the big DLS brakes back there. The remote shifting linkage is almost always sloppy and makes the already-iffy gearbox even more difficult to shift with precision. Forks are stiffer than those on the Dreams and don't respond as well to small bumps.

The 250cc Hawks are fairly uncommon in the United States because the more powerful (about 4 extra horsepower) 305s were offered side-by-side for an extra $30 or so. Unless a buyer was competing in a 250cc roadracing class, the choice between a CB72 and a CB77 was easy. If you come across a CB72 of any year, you have found a relatively rare machine, at least here in the United States.

CL72 & CL77 Scramblers (1962–67)

Scramblers are terrific fun to many enthusiasts because they sound so sweet with their long, straight exhaust pipes and because their seating position is fairly comfortable. The bike's style is an added draw. Its power is comparable to a Super Hawk because they share the same powerplant. Scramblers are a bit lighter overall than the Super Hawks and Dreams, due to the lack of an electric starter and the necessary high-amperage battery required to operate one. Because they are geared for acceleration in the dirt, the engines are much busier on the roads at highway speeds.

With a direct shift lever on the shift shaft, they shift more cleanly than the CBs. If you like to feel the bike you are riding, then the Scramblers are just the thing. They do have a pretty considerable high-frequency buzz just about everywhere on the bike, at most rpms.

Scramblers are more challenging to work on than Super Hawks and Dreams. If you are going to do much of anything on the left of the bike (service or replace the air filter or carburetor), the

Released in 1961, the 250-cc CB72 was always in the shadow of the 305-cc CB77. For just a few dollars extra, the CB77 offered four more horsepower in the same chassis. Only 3,479 CB72s were sold in the United States.

This factory photo of the 1966 CL77 shows the early slip-on muffler installed (later ones were welded on) and new 8-inch double-leading shoe brakes. *John Pavich*

pipes have to come off (you don't have to remove the pipes to service the clutch cover, though). Removal of the engine is more difficult as well. It has to be released out of the left side of the chassis rather than dropped down with a floor jack, as is the case with the CB and CA models. The 3.00x19 front and 3.50x19 rear tires are very hard to locate these days in anything that resembles the original tread pattern. Probably 80 percent of the unrestored Scramblers out there have chopped-off front fenders and fender stays. This little combo of parts can set you back some serious cash, especially for the alloy CL72 versions.

Released first as a 250cc machine in 1962, the Scrambler features weight-saving 7-inch SLS brakes and hubs, which are woefully underpowered for stopping on the street at almost any speed. The early CL77 engine is essentially a big-bore top end grafted onto the existing 250 Scrambler bottom end and left in the same type of 250 chassis, giving 4-5 more horsepower but accentuating the braking woes.

In 1966, Honda remedied this problem by adapting most of the front hub and the 8-inch DLS brakes from a CB450 onto the front of the alloy-fork versions of the 305cc Scramblers, with a matching DLS rear brake and hub combo, primarily relate to the CB77. This, along with some new alloy-fork slider assemblies, adds some heft to the newly revised machine, but the braking benefit is well worth the weight gain.

Unlike the relatively smooth CB72/77s, the Scramblers vibrate like crazy, causing lots of fracturing of the fenders, chain guards, side covers, mufflers, and batteries. A number of rubber-mounting modifications were employed to reduce buzzing vibration to both the rider and the affected components. Ultimately, the headlight mounts, seat, footpegs, muffler, and rear fenders were all cushioned with grommets and isolation mounts. It was an improvement, but never really a satisfactory upgrade. The forward frame down tube was probably the chief cause of the resonance. In the CB installation where the engine ties the frame together in front without the down tube, bikes suffer far less vibration-related damage. Bear in mind that these engines are 180 degree twins, spinning at 9-10,000 rpm and firing close together at first and then coasting on both pistons for one turn of the crankshaft before resuming. While the primary crankshaft balance is evened out by the alternating pistons, the uneven firing sequence sets up a secondary vibration pattern in the chassis.

CA72 & CA77 Dreams (1960–67)

The first Dreams to make it into the United States were CE71 Dream Sport machines from 1959–60 production. Based on the domestic C71 Dream, these machines feature separate oil tanks and crankshaft-mounted clutches from the original 1957-designed C70-C75s. According to parts books, only 390 CE71s were produced, surely one of the smallest production runs for a Honda

This is a first-year CSA77 Dream Sport model, released in 1960. *John Pavich*

street machine. The CE71's styling seems to have been penned by the same designer or team responsible for the CB92 Super Sport. This is especially noticeable in the fuel tank shape. At any rate, the CE71s are in short supply on the planet, and parts and bikes are at a premium.

For most Honda enthusiasts, the "real" Dreams came as the 1960 and later wet-sump machines, with the clutch moved back to the transmission shaft where it belonged in the first place. The 1961 and early 1962 Dreams had styling somewhat characteristic of the dry-sump models, but after 901 of the 1962 bikes were built, the styling was changed to the type seen on all later bikes. Many small detail changes were made through the production run, and other variations were sold outside the United States with sheet metal-type handlebars, rotary gearboxes, and "winkers" (turn signals) similar to the C100.

The 250cc version, CA72, is pretty rare in the United States for the same reason that the CB72 is: only a few dollars separated the 250 and the 305s, so the bigger version was almost always the choice. Japan and Europe had displacement breaks for taxation or licensing, and a 305cc machine usually put the owner into a larger bike category for tax purposes or for rider licensing. These restrictions were virtually unheard of in the United States, so the sales of 250cc bikes were minuscule in comparison to 305s.

With their 360 degree firing crankshafts, the 250-305 Dream engines are really quite smooth runners, especially in this chassis. Having high bars and reasonable seat height, they are quite comfortable around town too. Their squared-off styling draws stares as if they were from another planet, especially from the younger generation. Early bikes (1961–62) had stainless-steel mufflers, which were a real bonus. The suspension was very compliant over small bumps, but beyond that the driver would get a jolt. They are definitely the quietest bike around town, but at freeway speeds the intake roar is more noticeable than the exhaust.

CS77 Dream Sports, like this 1962 model, featured wet-sump engines and high-mounted exhaust systems on each side of the machine. Given the limitations of the chassis, these exhaust pipes were styling exercises, rather than serious offerings to the off-road enthusiasts. *AMA*

61

Wet-sump Dreams like this 1963 CA77 were available from 1961 to 1967. The 1961 and early 1962 models have seamless fuel tanks with central-mounted fuel fillers, twist throttles, and clamp-on mirrors. Engines were related to the CB/CL77, but had lower compression, alternate-firing 360-degree engines, and a single carburetor.

Dreams will keep you pretty clean if you ride through water due to the wide fenders, and there is plenty of leverage at the handlebars to correct your line through a corner. Considering they only have a single carburetor, most good-running Dreams perform as well with an averaged-sized passenger on board as when they are otherwise unencumbered. Their performance is quite surprising!

Dreams have a lot of inherent drawbacks, due to the nature of their original assignment. Touring in Japan didn't generally include long distances or high speeds, apparently, because the Honda 250-305 Dream isn't well suited to either task. Both models of Dreams share a single 22-millimeter carburetor, which restricts the top-end power potential, but they have strong midrange power and get great gas mileage. Dreams have lower-compression engines and wide-ratio gearboxes, so any idea of a fast-paced ride through the mountains will be put to rest very soon after you begin the test.

The leading-link front suspension has two limp dampers in front that match the pair at the rear, which only have about 2.5 inches of travel; after that, your only cushion is the 3.25x16 tires (tough to get in whitewalls now) and the thinly padded, suspended spring dual saddle. These seats are a little uncomfortable and your saddle time is limited to your tolerance. If you find a C77 with the solo seat, grab it! At highway speeds, the aforementioned dampering (or lack of it) situation affects the bike's ability to hold a line in a corner, as the wheels are literally jumping up and down on their own, without regard to where you would really like them to go. Those high, wide handlebars will come in handy here. They are fine around town or for short hops on the highway, but keep a lid on it in the twisty turns!

Like the Scramblers, the Dreams are often found with tweaked front fenders. Either people cut them off (and sometimes bobbed the rears, as well) or the trailing edge of the fender is rolled up and/or kinked. This usually happens if you ride off of a curb or try to jack up the front end with the lip of the fender. Dream front fenders seem to be more scarce than Scrambler's and although the (weld-on) rear fender sections were available from Honda, they are very hard to find. The resonant vibration of the Dream engine/chassis combination often hastens the demise of

Prior to 1964, badges on the CA77 read "Honda Dream 300," as shown on the 1962 bike on the left. Starting with the 1964 model, this was changed to "Honda 300," as shown on the 1965 model on the right. *Bill Silver/Peter Kendall collection*

the speedometers, taillight brackets, bulbs, and other bits and pieces if ridden on the freeway a great deal. Some owners have ridden well over 100,000 miles on their Dreams, though, so it isn't impossible to keep them alive for a good long time.

The newer wet-sump Dreams now had extra room under the right side cover, where the oil tanks used to be, to house the electrics comfortably. The rotary gearboxes, distributor caps, and crankshaft-mounted coils were gone. Now just one set of points controlled a double-ended ignition coil, which fired both spark plugs together on each stroke. They did retain the squared-off styling of the earlier models though. New higher, tubular handlebars gave riders more comfort than ever before.

The Dream series of bikes filled in the third leg of the 250-305cc triumvirate, and their unique, "square-everything" styling left no doubt that they were not just your average bike. Short-hop, in-city transport bikes, they were fitted with leading-link suspension in front, which was virtually undamped. The rear shocks (with 2.5 inches of rear travel) were similarly undamped, so the suspension easily yielded on little imperfections, but bottomed out on anything more substantial than a crosswalk paint stripe. All Dreams had 360-degree crankshafts, which fired their pistons on alternate strokes. This is the reverse of the situation with the CB/CL engines. While the primary balance was seemingly unfavorable, the firing sequence evened out the engine vibrations to a large extent. Dream engines had lowered compression (8.2:1 vs. 8.5:1) and had to breathe through a single, tiny 22-millimeter carburetor (same size for both 250 and 305s).

The new wet-sump 250-305cc Dreams featured 12-volt electrical systems, and the CA and CBs, of course, had electric starters. Just punch the button and you were running down the road. The whole range of machines represented an amazing breakthrough for that era and signaled a major shift in the level of performance of small motorcycles that could also be cost-effective to purchase and maintain.

CE71s like this 1960 version were early U.S.-spec "Dream Sport" models, featuring the dry-sump engine designs from the first-series 1957–1958 C70-C71 Dream models. Styling was similar to the 125-cc CB92. Honda used a CE71 to set a record for the Three-Flags run from Canada to Mexico in 1959. Some internal modifications were made to increase performance over the standard C71 Dream models. Only 390 were made, according to the parts books. *AMA*

This restoration of a rare 1959 CE71 shows details of this unique U.S.-only model. *Bill Orazio collection*

Mystery Models

Many domestic (Japanese) and "other market" variations of bikes were not sold in the United States. Just to satisfy the curious-minded and to dispel some rumors and myths about some of these models, they are covered briefly below.

CE71 Dream Sport (1959)

Brought into the U.S. as a sporting version of the standard C71 Dream, CE71 Dream Sports were advertised in 1959–60 magazine ads and promptly disappeared. According to the Honda parts manuals, only 390 were built. Were they cursed with problems that Honda didn't want to pursue or were they a stopgap machine to fill in until the CB72 and 77 Hawks and Super Hawks arrived in 1961? No one can say for sure, but rumor had it that Honda tried to buy back all of the CE71s produced. Despite the effort, a handful still exists in the United States.

CB72 Prototype (1960)

A book called *The Great Japanese Motorcycles* shows a single photo of a dry-sump 250 Hawk with a chromed, CB-styled fuel tank, long fork covers, and a host of interesting little tidbits. I've never seen the actual bike shown anywhere else in any publications, not even in the Honda Collector Hall Museum.

CP77 (1961–65)

The real confusion here is that some CP77s (referred to as CYP77s in the parts books) were factory Police bikes, and other CP77s

Honda Dream 250 300

The most dependable motorcycle

While most of the sales action focused on the Super Hawk and Scrambler models, the Dream still reached a segment of the growing market that sought smooth, quiet transportation capable of highway speeds.

appeared to be normal-looking CB77s, except that they were usually equipped with higher handlebars, turn signals, nonfolding footpegs, and the early-style 1961 taillight assy. Neither was officially imported here for sale, but more than a few are in the country, at least the non-Police versions. Some factory Police bikes have been found in Canada, and there was parts support for them there as well. None were ever sold in the United States.

Other than the external equipment cues and the CP77-0000001 serial numbers, you would assume that the non-Police machines were just regular CB77 models. And with the exception of the special bits, regular CB72/77 parts will fit these bikes.

The real (CYB) Police versions of the CB77 were made in two series, one with 17-inch wheels, oversized fenders, and Type 2 (360 degree firing crankshaft) motors. They have a single round speedometer (with lockable speedo needle for clocking speeders), turn indicators, crash-bar-mounted Patrol lights, and a cable-driven siren that is activated from a handlebar-mounted lever, which engages a swingarm-mounted drive unit that then contacts the rear tire. One or two bikes are in the United States, and a fully restored one is in the United Kingdom. Many were apparently sold in Southeast Asia and are now long gone.

By the way, when Honda uses a Y or YB designation for parts or bikes, it is an accessory item or accessory-equipped machine. The Y designation was often used in the parts systems for accessory items, but seldom as a model, except for the road racing CYB350 and the CYB77 Police bikes. To give you an idea of how many variations of parts there were for just the CB72/77s, the European version of the parts manual, covering all models, has 281 pages whereas the U.S. edition has about 80.

CL300 (1968)

You probably already figured it out, but the CL300 is a CL77 with turn signals, solid pegs, late-model forks, chrome fenders, and the late, oval-shaped taillight. This little quirk in the model series seems to be a result of leftover Scramblers at the end of the 1967 production, sold in 1968 along with the new CB/CL250/350s. The few that have surfaced here have been equipped similarly and seem to be domestic bikes. They look just like the last of the CL77s, but with the aforementioned differences in equipment and the CL300 frame and engine number sequences. So if you happen across one, it is real! Perhaps Honda decided to make all of its model designators the same in 1968.

Precious little on a Dream was round, including the speedometers. *Peter Kendall collection*

This stylish fender tip, a genuine Honda accessory, was created exclusively for Dream and Benly models. *Peter Kendall collection*

C72 & C77 Dream (1960–65)

A source at American Honda's motorcycle public relations department checked old sales figures and discovered that more than 72,000 Super Hawks were sold in the United States alone. More than 76,000 Scramblers were also sold here, as it was the prime market for the dual-purpose machines. Dreams were sold at about 10-15,000 per year for seven years, so you can see that quite a few 250-305 twins were delivered to the American market. These continue to be the most sought-after series of Honda motorcycles.

Although the 1961–67 series of Dreams, Super Hawks, and Scramblers looked pretty much the same through the years, Honda made numerous detail improvements during the production runs, and you must pay careful attention when ordering parts for them. Building a bike from several similar-appearing parts-bikes can end in disappointment and confusion for the novice restorer.

These bikes are generally Japanese domestic bikes, brought in by servicemen in the 1960s. Domestic Dreams have rotary gearboxes (press down 1-2-3-4-N-1-2-3-4), which are convenient for stop-and-go traffic in Japan, or maybe New York City. They are usually found with solo seats and a rear rack. A buddy seat pad can be quickly attached to the rack to carry a friend. These machines may be found with either sheet-metal handlebars or conventional tubular versions and turn signals, of course.

Modern Twins: CB350 & CL350 (1968–73)

By the late 1960s, Honda's line of the Dream, the Super Hawk, and the Scrambler was outdated. The basic design of these models had been around for almost 10 years, and Honda had some new technological tricks up its sleeves. The bikes that replaced the Honda twin trio were two all-new machines, the road-oriented CB350 and the CL350 Scrambler.

The CB/CL350s were released in 1968, followed in 1969 by the SL350 Motosport series machine (still with electric-starting). The 350s were a big-bore version of the basic 250cc bikes sold in Japan, Europe, and the U.K. Other than larger top-end components (pistons, rings, head gasket, cylinders, and different cylinder head machining) including carburetion, they were the same machine weight-wise.

The newfound power of the extra displacement (actually only an additional 20cc over the 305 series) was rated at 36 horsepower on the CB versions and 33 horsepower on the CL Scramblers versus the previous 28 horsepower for the 305s. The redesign featured updated cylinder head breathing via larger valves, reshaped combustion chambers, and improved porting. There was now a two-piece cylinder head with a separate camshaft carrier and replaceable cam-bearing holders.

Everyone praised the new five-speed gearbox, although it was still being operated by remote linkage, adding a lot of slop to the system. There was news inside the horizontally split bottom end too. The old "stretchy" primary chain gives way to a double pair of straight-cut

Honda's hot-selling 350 twins were drawing to a close in 1972. There were some internal engine modifications along the way, but the basic design was carried through with primarily cosmetic changes.

CL350 Airborne! This Honda sales brochure demonstrates the power and strength of Honda's new model Scrambler. Don't try this at home, kids!

gears, reducing driveline lash. Additionally, a new plunger-type oil pump is driven off of an eccentric, machined in the back of the outer clutch basket.

The newly applied rubber-diaphragm constant velocity (CV) carburetors helps control the fuel more accurately, but is somewhat abrupt when the driver rolls off the throttle. These new mixers feature primary and secondary main jets, with sealing duties handled by various-sized O-rings versus the old flat gaskets. With CV carburetors, you could grab a big handful of throttle because you were only opening the butterflies while the diaphragms were sensing the various differential pressures, which ultimately affected the rate of opening of throttle slides.

The spark advancer unit was still attached to the camshaft, but was now mounted on the outboard end, rather than a part of the cam sprocket, as in the days of old (250-305). This allowed for easy maintenance of the ignition system and more accurate overall spark timing.

Overall, one is hard pressed to find more than a handful of fasteners that are the same as the 250-305s, such was the complete revamping of the machine. With new ideas, however, there are often a few teething problems which mostly center around the camshafts (either not properly heat-treated or fail due to lack of oil) and the cam chain tensioner. The original tensioner was a hydraulic type that relaxed when the engine was off, causing a racket on restart. This was rectified with a recall for a new spring-loaded, mechanical replacement, more in the style of the 250-305s. The camshafts had a lot of overlap on the first models and Honda tamed them down a little by trimming 10 degrees off of the overlap. This change required some carburetion changes, which cover most of the midrange and high-speed settings, so one must be selective if changing carburetors from one series to another.

Oiling problems surfaced with gasket deterioration problems of both the clutch and dyno covers. Little chunks of gasket material from unsupported areas float up in the oil stream to block critical passageways, causing seizing of the camshaft bearings and damage to the rocker arms. If you hear a lot of upper-end noises in one of these engines and you are unable to adjust the valve clearances with the eccentric shafts, then your cams and rockers are history.

The frame is a double-cradled affair, combining tubular and pressed-steel sections to provided a rugged and stable platform for the suspension. Brakes were a DLS front and SLS rear, until the final CB350G model, which featured a single-piston disc front brake. Rear shocks are a DeCarbon style (gas-filled dampers), which were supposed to reduce the aeration of the damping oil. While better than the CB77 shocks, they are not a shining attribute of the handling package and are often replaced with aftermarket shocks.

Servicing the battery is a different experience, depending on the series of bike. Early models have a rear hinged seat with a prop rod. The K3 and later machines have a more common side-hinged arrangement, but the seat corner or edging always seems to want to scratch the fuel tank during removal. The seats can't swing very far over due to interference of the rear wraparound grab rails on the 1973 models, making the situation worse.

A last-year 1973 CB350 "G" model with the disc brake is a good example of the best of the CB350s. Over the years, the forks were refined and the bike seemed a little more agreeable, but it was still turning 8,000 rpm at 75 miles per hour and gave your hands a good "buzz" after a short ride at that speed. Honda's sole attempt to mitigate the shakes on the 350s was a rubber cushion, as a part of the top motor mount, which may have helped, but the rest of the motor was bolted in solidly to the frame. Although the 350 engines were destroked to 50.6 millimeters from the 305's 54 millimeters, the 4-millimeter larger pistons seem to have created a greater overall level of shaking. The CB350s power peak is listed at 10,500 rpm and the CL/SLs at around 9, 000 rpm, whereas the 250-305s peak at 8,500 and redline at 9,000. Virtually all 350s suffer from cracked, vibration-damaged mufflers, and new or even serviceable used replacements are getting quite scarce.

Eventually, Honda bored its mid-sized street twin engines out to 67 millimeters (356cc), using the same 50.6-millimeter 350 stroke in the 360T engine series, but once high-revving parallel twins get out to the 350cc size, there isn't much one can do to smooth them out short of counterbalancers or rubber-mounting the entire motor. Just as their forerunners, the 360s were shakers of low-amplitude and high-frequency. The

The first generation replacement for the CL77 Scrambler is this CL350K0, with an all-new engine design and a five-speed transmission. *Troyce Walls*

After an exhaust-system makeover in 1970, the CL350s made the most of the tooling costs and received only cosmetic changes for the most part. Mechanically identical to the CB350s, they soldiered on in parallel with the street bikes until their replacements, the six-speed CB/CL360s, arrived in 1974.

problem wasn't successfully solved until the dual-counterbalanced 1978 Hawk series engines were introduced.

The 350 engines were the best that Honda could do, given all of the design and market factors present at that time, and an increasing number of them are being resurrected and restored. They were one of Honda's top-selling bikes in the era before the inline-fours were brought to market; and they were the foundation of the continuing motorcycle market explosion of the late 1960s and early 1970s.

CB360T, CL360T, & CJ360T (1974–77)

Honda's midsized street twins of the mid-1970s are variations of the again-revised single overhead cam (SOHC) 2-valve design concept, now featuring 356cc and a new six-speed transmission. The newly designed 1974 CB360T was the new street model, and of course there are CL Scrambler versions, plus a stripped down, cafe-styled CJ360T version (with a 2-into-1 exhaust) that languished in dealers' showrooms. Of all the Honda street twins, the 360T was the only one that never raced in competition or was modified to any extent. These machines are definitely dependable, rugged, and mild-mannered but never had high-performance credentials. Lasting from 1974 to

The CB360 arrived in 1974 as a replacement for the aging CB350. In addition to a modest displacement increase, the new bike feature a six-speed transmission.

Showing a bit of cafe-racer influence, the CJ360 was lightened by deleting the electric starter, centerstand, one of the transmission gearsets and the disc brake, while receiving a new two-into-one exhaust system and color-matched plastic front fender. As the CJ360 sold head-to-head with the CB400F (which was struggling then, too), most potential customers came to an obvious conclusion: the Four is More!

1977 in CB form (1976–77 as CJs) and only from 1974 to 1975 as CLs, they signified the end of the two-valve, midsized street twin-series machines.

CB/CM400 and 450 (1978–85)

In 1978, the quaking, shaking 360s gave way to the new, smooth, counterbalanced (due to a 360-degree plain-bearing crankshaft) SOHC, three-valve per cylinder Hawk 400-series machines. This was the first series of street bikes with CDI pointless ignitions and a HyVo, link-style cam chain in addition to the automotive-style, plain-bearing lower end.

These new models began as CB400T/TII and CB400A (automatic) in 1978 and then became CM400A (automatic), C (custom), and E (economy) models as the custom-look (stepped seats, shorty mufflers, and pulled-back handlebars) machines joined the lineup in 1979. There was a sporty version of the Hawk 400-series machines (CB400T Hawk) in 1980–81, enlarged to 450cc for the 1982 season and accompanied by a CB450SC Nighthawk version that was again going cruiser-style

The CM400A was released in 1978 as part of the CB400T Hawk-series machines; the "A" stands for automatic transmission. Simply select L for Low or D for Drive! CM versions were "Custom"-styled. Engine capacity was increased to 450 cc in 1982. *AMA*

The CB450 Nighthawk 450 featured an enlarged version of the earlier 400-cc Hawk-series engines.

through the final year of 1986. All of the CM-series bikes were enlarged in 1982 to 450cc for the remaining two years of production.

Spurred by success of the 250 Rebels, Honda dusted off the old CM450 engine and rewrapped it in Rebel clothing in response to the critics of the 250's low power output. The six-speed, three-valve engine propels the low, lightened 450 along quite smartly, but the bubble burst after the 250 Rebel's novelty wore off, and the rather expensive 450s languished in dealer showrooms.

Like its earlier effort with the CB750As (1976–787), Honda fielded CM400A and CM450A versions of the little twin, again using a two-speed (Low-Drive) transmission. And again the marketplace turned up its collective nose at Honda's efforts. Honda fans who drive automatics usually drive Accords!

DOHC Twins: CB450 & CB500T (1965–76)

Released late in 1965, the new CB450 Black Bomber was Honda's first DOHC production motorcycle and featured a novel torsion-bar valve spring system. Much of the bike's chassis was related to the CB77 in design and function, so not much new ground was broken there. The engines were a masterpiece of technology, breathing through new CV-style carburetors lifted off of the Honda S600 sports cars. A five-speed transmission would have been a crowning touch, but was not included initially. Early bikes suffer some problems with oil flow, damaging the expensive twin-cam top ends, and carburetion was reworked

Christened "Black Bomber," the CB450 shook up the motorcycle world after its introduction in late 1965 with its high-tech double overhead cam, two-valve motor, featuring torsion-bar valve spring control and new CV vacuum-piston carburetors. Unfortunately Honda left out a much-needed five-speed transmission. The first generation of Honda's "big twins" are very collectible models. *AMA*

several times in the beginning years.

When ridden, the CB450 feels like a top-heavy, big-bore Super Hawk, fitted with high handlebars and sliding around on unacceptable OEM tires. The tires were Dunlops, licensed and made in Japan. The front tire had a chunky rib design with a mind of its own. Early road test reports were not particularly kind to this bike, which was a slap in the face for Honda after all of its efforts to break into the "big bike" performance market. "You can't beat cubic inches" (or ccs), as the saying goes, and with all of the advanced design features, Honda still wasn't in the game with the 444cc machine.

After two years, the four-speed bikes gave way to new updated five-speed bikes, and a CL-style 450 Scrambler was introduced to complete the line of dual-purpose models begun with the 1962 CL72, 250cc Scrambler. Honda did make a D-model Scrambler CB450 four-speed bike, which was a precursor to the CL450, except the pipes were high on both sides, rather than the usual crossover and sweep up the left configuration. Whole D-kits were available to convert a CB450 Bomber into a CB450D machine. Both the bikes and the D-kit parts are in high demand now and are hard to find. It was up to the CB450s to hold the "Honda Big Bike" reins until 1969 and they did the best they could, considering all the competition at that time.

One must remember that during this time, the Honda factory was waging war on the world GP circuits with their multicylinder roadrac-

Honda did not offer an out-of-the-crate Scrambler version of the "Black Bomber," but you could build your own with a "D" model conversion kit, available from your dealer.

ing machines, competing in the 50, 125, 250, 350, and 500cc classes. This was a huge expense and drain on the engineering talent pool, as racing was a primary focus for Mr. Honda. Little did we know what was cooking on the back burner of Honda's R&D department during the late 1960s . . . the CB750!

The CB450s did pick up the 750's front disc-brake system in 1970 and shared some of the styling cues from its big brother too, but sales weakened with the presence of the powerful, popular four-cylinder machine in the marketplace. The DOHC 450-designed engine's last gasp of life was as a stroked CB500T, sold (barely) in 1975–76 (no CL versions of that bike). Buyers were turned off by the brown seat covers, a bulky crossover chamber between the headers, and the extra vibration of the enlarged engine. Magazine road tests were brutal and rude to the new model and the public responded in kind. The bikes were certainly no sales matchup for a CB550 four, which was a direct competitor for the midsize sales dollars, and the CB450 quietly passed away into oblivion.

CB450 Four-Speed Black Bomber (1965–67)

Honda began to show the new CB450 in 1965. The elegantly complex 444cc, 43-horsepower engine featured a number of new design features including dual OHCs driven by a long, 128-link cam chain (vs. 94 on a CB77), torsion-bar valve springs, gear-driven primary drive, and CV carburetors, all on a roller-bearing crankshaft that would spin up to a 9,000 rpm redline. Valve clearance was only .002

In 1968, Honda introduced the next generation 450 machine after the Black Bomber, now offered in colors other than black! New features included more horsepower, a five-speed transmission, separate gauges, chrome fenders, and new styling that brought a more modern look to this double overhead cam twin. *Troyce Walls*

inches and accomplished by a system of eccentric shafts that changed the relationship of the rockers to the camshafts, similar to the 350 twins. The system is so solid and reliable that the CR450 road racers would turn up to 12,000 rpm without valve float.

The 450 chassis is a cradle-type, surrounding the power plant and including a front down tube, which was new for a Honda twin other than the CL72/77 Scramblers. The front suspension and brake were still in the CB77 pattern, but the rear brakes were now actuated by a rod and were of SLS design, which is more effective overall than the DLS rear of the Super Hawk. Rear shocks are dead copies of the CB72/77s, but were upgraded for the extra weight and load capacity of the machine. Overall, the CB450 weight is about 60 pounds heavier than the Super Hawk. Tires were upgraded to 3.25x18 in the front and 3.50x18 in the rear. Top speed was rated at 106 miles per hour.

Honda's new "big twin" struck another blow to the heart of the British bike industry, with the usual oil-tight horizontal split crankcases, electric starters, bright 12-volt electrics, and the Honda reputation for reliability and service support. There were early-model teething problems in the oil pumps and erratic carburetion. Honda determined the causes and acted swiftly to ensure customer satisfaction. The oil pumps were a real concern as a localized oil flow in the original design pumps caused breakage of the pump filter screens, allowing debris to block critical oil feed passages to the upper end and causing lots of damage to expensive parts. Modifications to the pump cured the problem, and the same basic design carried on for the rest of the production.

Out on the road, the wide-ratio gearbox is compensated by the high-torque engine, but once in top gear, it cries out for a fifth ratio. As busy as they sound, they can play that tune for hours at a time, if the rider is up to the task. If you really want to ride, it is always recommended that you replace the rear dampers with a set of aftermarket units (especially if you are taking a passenger). To truly enjoy the bike, plan on locating something better than the OEM shocks, particularly if they

The K2-and-later CB450 versions mimic the larger CB750s in styling cues, and benefited from the inclusion of the 750's front disc brake in 1970. *Bill Orazio*

have more than a few thousand miles on them.

There is currently a strong movement to obtain and restore Black Bombers, primarily because they were the "first" edition of their kind and because people actually like the bike! From an overall performance standpoint, the next-generation K1 models, with upgraded five-speed transmissions and improved breathing on the top end, are far more functionally advanced, and to some, even more attractive. Looking around today, though, there are far fewer "Toaster Tank" (sorry BMW!) CB450K1 five-speeders around than the clunkier four-speed versions. Overall, an especially attractive CB450 to ride and own is the 1970–72 (K2-K4) edition, with the front disc brake and the early-CB750 styling cues.

If you must have a CB450, get a good one to begin with, as the restoration costs of the motor alone will be staggering. As with most of the other twins, the mufflers suffer from rot and replacements are scarce, plus there are a number of styles and variations of mufflers. The early bikes have at least three styles, including two-piece and one-piece units, with or without a set of additional forward-mounted triangle brackets.

Always obtain a copy of the parts manual for any bike you select. This will give you a frame of reference for which parts go where and how many parts there are altogether. As is the case with all Honda models, there were big and small changes, and you need to be aware of them during the repair or restoration process.

CL450 Scramblers were the last of the CL Scrambler line, which began in 1962 with the original CL72s. Paintwork, seats, decals, and exhaust systems changed virtually every year to separate each version, although they remained the same mechanically. *Bill Orazio*

CB-500T

Candy Red   Metallic Brown

Honda tried to stretch a little more life from the venerable CB450s in 1976 by stroking the engine to 500 cc. Brown seat covers and unsightly exhaust balance chambers turned off prospective buyers who opted instead for the faster, smoother CB550 Fours.

CP450 White Bomber & CB450 Red Bomber (1966-67)

Two rare variations are the Red and White Bombers. The existence of actual factory red bikes is often debated, but red shock covers were listed in the parts books. This could have been an error, as no other parts were listed with red options. A few individuals claim to own red bikes, but none have yet been authenticated. White Bombers, however, are real factory-built Police bikes, but they are in very scarce supply. The CP450 four-speed White Bomber is basically a CB450 with interesting accessories, including a six-position ignition switch and a single round speedometer with locking mechanism for the needle at any speed. One could certainly trace a good deal of the heritage of the CB450 to the CB77, even though the part numbers are different. They do share common fork seals, in one instance. Riding the 450 gives the same impression as a big-bore CB77, except for an awareness of a higher center of gravity and a little more footprint on the pavement. As far as the chassis goes, the overall suspension feel and handling is much like the Hawk and similarly undamped. The clutch is grabby and unhappy about releasing first thing in the morning. Once warmed and cycled through a few gear changes, it settles down to something more palatable.

Only 25 of these factory-built CB450 Police models were imported into the United States. Apparently U.S. law enforcement officials couldn't quite make the leap from a 1,200-cc Harley-Davidson Police motorcycle to a 444-cc Honda bike, and after the initial introduction, they were withdrawn from the marketplace. A later five-speed model was sold in other countries. *AMA*

V-twins

Honda's history with V-twins is relatively short, although they have made some significant motorcycles powered by this configuration. The company first brought out a production V-twin in the CX500, a somewhat odd motorcycle that morphed into a touring bike and the company's Buck Rogers-esque entry into the turbocharging frenzy of the mid-1980s. The Ascot received a version of the engine which, considering the flat track styling of the model, seemed logical. None of these bikes were terrifically successful, although each attracted a core of enthusiasts.

When Honda put their V-twin technology into a high-tech chassis to create the Hawk GT, they had truly found a good home for the design. Unfortunately, despite the bike's attractive mix of handling and torque, the public remained nonplused.

Honda's Super Hawk, an open-class twin in a light, narrow, sporting chassis, was a winner. The bike did all the things a sportbike should do, in a magically easy-to-use fashion. The public, perhaps taught to accept V-twins by Ducati's one-two punch of racing prowess and popular exotica, took to the Super Hawk with abandon.

The RC51 promises the same, with racetrack prowess to match the Super Hawk's streeting sensibility. With a limited production run, it's unlikely that many of these will make it into Joe Pocket Rocket's hands.

The custom versions of the CX500 V-Twins were offered for the second year in 1980. This "custom" styling took over several product lines in the 1979–1983 era, starting with the CM200 and ending with the CB1000C. *AMA*

CX500 and CX650 (1978–83)

For 1978, Honda introduced its first transverse V-twin, the CX500. The shaft-drive 80-degree V-twin was a midsized street bike designed to be a companion to the GL1000 Gold Wings. The CX500s were often compared to Moto-Guzzis, because of the transverse (crossways) 80 degree V-twin configuration and the pushrod valve actuation. The CX500 had four valves per cylinder, rather than the Guzzi's two-valve heads. The controversial Bat Wing styling of the 1978–79 Standard models, particularly around the headlight nacelle, drew complaints and made the addition of aftermarket fairings difficult. The later CX500D (Deluxe) models came with cleaned-up chromed steel fork ears, putting the Bat Wing controversy to rest.

The first models were plagued with cam chain tensioner failures, corrected through a series of recalls. Some crankshaft bearings were incorrectly fitted at the factory as well, in 1978. The other persistent failures have been the alternator stators and/or ignition triggers, all located inside the back of the motor, requiring removal of the powerplant and then accessed by removing the rear engine case. These bikes are revered in England and other countries as reliable courier motorcycles, racking up over 100,000 miles with minimal repair expense.

Honda revised the bike into a cruiser-style in 1979, with the CX500 Custom (its first Custom-styled street bike) and added the GL Silver Wing and Silver Wing Interstate touring versions in 1981.

CX500TC (1982)

When turbocharging became all the rage (Kawasaki GPZ 750 Turbo and the Suzuki 850 Turbo) in the early 1980s, Honda responded with a stunning, limited-production CX500T sport bike, which topped out at over 125 miles per hour. Then, in 1983 (after a major redesign of the CX500s into CX650s, including a 97-horsepower CX650T), Honda dropped the entire line of machines as they readied the new line of water-cooled V-fours.

Other V-Twins

Honda produced several longitudinal V-twin–powered bikes. The engine first appeared in 1983 in the VT500 Ascot, and variations were used in the Hawk GT, the VT500 Custom, the VLX600 Cruiser, the PC800, and the 750cc Transalp. Of these

Honda fired the first shot in the factory turbo wars in April 1982 with the hand-assembled CX500TC. Yamaha countered a month later with its XJ650L, a turbocharged version of the 650 Seca. Suzuki brought out the XN85, a turbocharged 650-cc machine, later that year, and in September 1983, Kawasaki introduced a turbocharged 750. It seemed everyone would build turbocharged motorcycles in the years to come. Not true–only 3,000 CX500TC machines were made. *AMA*

The CX650TC replaced the CX500TC for the 1983 model year. The 650-cc version had a new fuel injection management system and about 20 more horsepower. Bodywork was injection-molded ABS vs. the hand-laid fiberglass pieces of the CX500T. When the boost is up, it can humble many 1,000cc bikes in a roll-on competition. *AMA*

models, the Ascot and the Hawk are the most collectible. Finding original, low-mile versions of these bikes is getting increasingly difficult, as they were produced for only two to three years.

VT500 Ascot (1983–84)

The VT500 Ascot is a direct descendant of the single-cylinder FT500 Ascot. The longitudinal 90-degree firing V-twin engines featured a SOHC, three-valve heads, and offset crankpins. VT500s are solid, reliable machines. The engines are durable and the maintenance-free shaft-drives provide years of worry-free service.

Honda had only limited success with the original VT500 Ascot. Trying to link a shaft-driven street bike to the famous Southern California racing circuit was a stretch, to say the least. The existence of the single-cylinder FT500 Ascot further confused the issue, and ultimately, the VT500 did not sell well. Bikes could be found at dealerships for fire-sale prices in the mid-1980s.

Honda used the Ascot name on two completely different types of machines: this liquid-cooled, shaft-driven, pseudo-flat-track-styled V-twin and an XL500-based four-valve single.

Hawk GT (1988–91)

In 1988 the ghost of the VT500 would return as a high-tech, beautifully constructed bike: the Hawk GT (aka the NT650). With Ducati sales on the rise, riders seemed to be showing more interest in V-twin configuration machinery, so Honda responded with a half-old, half-new release in the form of the Hawk GT. The chassis was all new and wondrous: alloy frame, single-sided swingarm rear suspension, beautiful cast alloy wheels, and a dry weight of 399 pounds. The powerplant was a mix of ideas, based on the basic VT500. The heads were still basic VT500 three-valve, twin-plug design, fitted with bigger carburetion and different cams. The six-speed transmission was dropped in favor of a five-speed. The drive-shaft was jettisoned for a conventional chain, which wrapped around the VFR-styled rear swingarm. The nonadjustable front suspension was lifted from the 750 Nighthawk street bikes. The result was a good motor in a brilliant chassis, and it became an effective platform for Twin-series roadracers.

Sold for only three years, the NT650 is the cheapest way to experience the wonders of the single-sided swingarm chassis. Next above the NT650 is the VFR750R or an RC-30. The single-sided swingarm is a wonder of casting and machining wizardry and offers the added benefit of simple, clean, and quick rear wheel removal. The front and rear disc brakes do a fine job of stopping on the street, but those of the racing persuasion have found that the front end off of an F-2 CBR600 bolts on with minimal modification, offering better brakes and bigger forks.

Hawk GTs respond well to a host of modifications. Seats, exhaust pipes, and mods to the somewhat mild engine are quite popular and can transform the nimble but mildly powered Hawk into a backroad terror or class-competitive racer.

Because the cylinder head castings were certified with EPA in the VT500 configuration, Honda elected to leave them in place on the 650, and this is its main stumbling block to performance. However, the Two Brothers racing team won a national championship with a heavily modified Hawk GT, against all comers in the 750cc and up classes. Today, the bikes continue to have a cult following, and the prices for a clean low-miles bike easily run $2,500-up.

The Hawk GT sports machine, which used the VT500 motor in a VFR-type chassis equipped with a beautiful cast-alloy, single-sided rear swing arm, was produced from 1988 to 1991. *AMA*

If you are going to compete with the big boys, you have to have big toys! While the VF1100C V-4 Magna had more horsepower than the American-brand cruisers ever dreamed of, it didn't sound or look like the big twin cruisers. The answer was to build a bigger twin; thus, the VT1100C was born in 1985. With its shaft-drive and twin-plug, three-valve engine, the Shadow 1100 followed in the mold of the rest of the VT "Custom" lineup, but now with some cubic inches to brag about.

Even in stock condition, the NT650 is an enjoyable ride for most riders. The wide rims and powerful front brake give great traction and control. The small-port heads give lots of low and midrange torque. Those who have cut their teeth on high-revving inline fours will be surprised at how responsive the motor can be around town and in the canyons. Rear seating is adequate for short hops, but the passenger pegs are mounted high, causing discomfort in a short time. The low-rise clip-on type handlebars are comfortable, as long as the wind is putting a little pressure on your chest at speed to take some weight off your wrists. Handlebar controls fall readily to hand and the push-to-cancel turn signal switch works well if your gloves aren't too bulky. Steering response is terrific and the bike will lean over in the turns without dragging much of anything.

If you were born and bred on inline fours, you owe it to yourself to find a Hawk GT and at least give it a test ride. The slender shape, handsome styling, light weight, and rigid chassis will probably win your heart in minutes. The NT650 left a gap in the lineup in 1992, but the name and the concept were born again in the late 1990s with the release of the 1000cc Super Hawk, a 100-horsepower machine, still in the low 400-pound bracket. Finally, Honda enthusiasts got their wish for a lightweight machine with some real power, but for most riders, the Hawk GT can give a healthy taste of the Super Hawk performance, at just a fraction of the price.

In order to avoid the federally mandated tariff on motorcycles over 700cc, Honda reduced the engine size on its 1984 VT750 twin to 700cc.

Honda responded to the demand for more "cruiser-type" machines with this 500-cc version of the Shadow family.

RC-51 (2000)

Honda's latest racing/street model is the RC-51, released in the spring of 2000. This bike is certain to set the performance world on its ear, offering incredible performance at the bargain-basement price of $9,999. With limited availability and an impressive spec sheet, these bikes are sure to become collectible immediately and only gain in value.

Chapter 6

The Classic Four-Cylinders

In the late 1960s, at the urging of American Honda's Bob Hansen, Honda R&D began to develop a new class of motorcycle for the American market. Hansen had said that the U.S. market was primed for a large displacement, multicylinder machine, based on Honda's racing successes of the 1960s. We will never know for sure whether this was all it took to launch the project, but soon after, Honda sent Mr. Hansen some photos and information about a 750-cc-sized four-cylinder machine, which, as a test mule, was shown with a CB450 drum brake in front.

The rest of the story is motorcycling history, of course, triggering the creation of machines like the Kawasaki Z-1 in 1973 in response and a flood of inline motors from 250cc fours to 1047cc six-cylinder sizes. This configuration remains with us today as the standard for most 600cc and larger street machines. Honda's stroke of genius in the CB750 was the death-knell for the British motorcycle industry, a slow death that began in 1961 when the CB72 Hawk was introduced. The days of pushrods and long-stroke parallel twins with unsupported center bearings drew to a close not long after the release of the 64 horsepower CB750 Four.

This early Honda promotional photo shows a preproduction version of the CB750, used in some early magazine ads. Note the unusual side cover vents and emblems, the lack of an emblem on the generator cover, and missing heat shields on the mufflers. *Bill Orazio*

The new SOHC inline four was a revelation to the motorcycle industry. New for Honda was a plain-bearing crankshaft, their first move away from the usual ball/roller-bearing engines of the past. The hydraulic front disc brake was an appropriate addition to such a heavy and fast machine.

CB750 (1969–82)

Because Americans rode CB750s so fast, the early ones had some problems not anticipated at the factory, and some were downright dangerous. Broken drive-chains that created broken engine cases were the leading item in the list of priority repairs and recalls. There are 100 pages of technical service and parts bulletins pertaining to the modifications and maintenance of these early bikes.

When the CB750 K1 series bikes were released, the carburetors had inherited a push-pull throttle cable system, while new drive chains and sprocket sizes mitigated the faults of the previous editions. Complaints were down, sales were up, and 750s were seen everywhere, touring, commuting, and racing. In 1973 alone, some 60,000 CB750s were sold. At this time, previous to the release of the GL1000 Gold Wings, the CB750 was the bike for touring, and thousands were outfitted with aftermarket fairings, luggage racks, crashbars, saddlebags, footboards, accessory lights, radios, and all of the other pieces of the period. If they weren't out touring America, then they were at racetracks as roadracers or drag bikes. Russ Collins of *RC Engineering* campaigned a triple-engine CB750 drag bike to show what could be done with a CB750 engine. George Kerker pioneered the 4:1 exhaust system design, and similar systems were offered by numerous manufacturers to replace the stock 4:4 systems for

The mighty CB750 Four, with its powerful, single overhead cam inline four-cylinder engine, took the motorcycle world by storm in 1969. It was even equipped with a hydraulic front disc brake. Smooth and capable of 125 miles per hour, the 480-pound (dry) machine was the model of good manners in town and ruled the world in 1970, when it captured the Daytona 200 crown. *AMA*

By 1974, Honda's once-mighty CB750 had been eclipsed by Kawasaki's Z-1.

CB-750F

Candy Red   Solid Yellow

The 1975 CB750F was the first of the four-into-one-exhaust-equipped Supersport versions of the single overhead cam bikes. A rear disc brake was added, along with all new bodywork. Wire wheels continued until 1977, when the revised bikes with black-painted motors and Comstar wheels came out. *Bill Orazio*

more power or to replace the expensive OEM systems, which often rotted out due to condensation damage, were crash damaged, or just to make more room for saddlebags due to the upswept design of the original mufflers. Finding correct OEM mufflers remains one of the greatest challenges for restorers of many Honda models, especially the CB750.

The final edition of the CB750F Super Sport was released in 1977. The CB750F 1977–78 models featured all-black painted engines tweaked with big-valve heads, more radical cams, factory 4:1 exhaust, Comstar wheels, and triple-disc brakes. The factory muffler system gives the exhaust

86

Honda's CB750A featured an automatic transmission, earning it the name "Hondamatic" from Honda's marketing types.

"Honda is ready for you today," proclaimed this 1977 ad for the ill-fated CB750A Hondamatic. Honda may have been ready for a motorcycle with an automatic transmission, but apparently the motorcycling public was not, and the bike sold poorly.

a more muted baritone note. The EPA-mandated carburetion produces a little lean spot in part-throttle cruising, and the CB750Fs are a little more cold-blooded first thing in the morning. Honda massaged about 6 more horsepower out of the original design, and that is always a good thing. The forks were more compliant, the triple-disc brakes were a vast improvement, and the entire bike was more supple and refined. These were sweet bikes, but the handwriting was on the wall: DOHC-engine machines from Suzuki, Kawasaki, and Yamaha were overshadowing the SOHC legacy, and it was time to retire this engine design and move forward.

Riding the CB750

Most baby-boomers can vividly recall their first sighting of a CB750. I remember my first experience just sitting on the tall, hefty machine and wondering what Mr. Honda had wrought this time. I flipped the petcock to the "on" position, gently hit the starter button, and beheld an amazing sound coming to my ears. Four 184cc cylinders (736cc total) were alternately cackling into four curvaceous mufflers and resonating off the garage walls. As I gingerly accelerated through the lower gears, I was awed by the smoothness and precision of the gearbox and controls. When I delicately applied the front brake to test its responsiveness, it gave just as much stopping power as requested, no more and no less. Despite the height and top-heavy feeling, I felt at home quickly.

After riding lightweights for years, it took me a while to adjust fully to the handling and power of the machine, but it wasn't long before I was going over 100 miles per hour on a daily basis, just to feel and hear the powerful engine hit its "sweet spot" and wait for the next gear. Impromptu drag races and roll-ons with friends' Brit twins and even H-D Super Glides were no contest once the 750's power curve kicked in. When my buddy's Triumph 650 Daytona was panting at 90 miles per hour, I was still in the top of third with two gears to go. The Super Glide guy was so determined to dust me off at a stoplight challenge that, in his haste, he almost destroyed his transmission. Even at 110 miles per hour, packing double, it was never a contest. I just had to downshift a gear if necessary and nail the throttle, and it was "bye-bye"! Original CB750s are always a joy to see, ride, and hear.

Since Honda could no longer claim its CB750 topped the high-performance heap, this 1974 ad stresses the communal aspect of motorcycling.

CB500-550–650s (1971–82)

Honda's stunning success with the CB750-series SOHC four-cylinder bikes led to a scaled-down version that was suitable for more people. The CB500 four, introduced in 1971, was lighter (409 pounds), lower, shorter (2 inches less wheelbase), and more nimble, with all the features and advantages of the larger bike: smooth four-cylinder engine (50 horsepower at 9,000 rpm), five-speed transmission, electric-starting, front disc brake, and so on. The engine was based on a wet-sump design, rather than the 750's dry-sump version with separate oil tank. The primary drive off of the crankshaft was with a Hy-Vo link plate chain, avoiding the double-roller chains of the big brother 750.

The 1971–73 CB500K0-K2 versions were visually identical, other than some changes to the taillights, instruments, and paint schemes. In 1974 the CB500s became CB550K0, then K1, K'76, K'77, and K'78 carrying the basic CB500 styling cues over and wearing the same trumpet-tipped four-pipe exhaust system. The CB500s were known to be rather thirsty, so the CB550 carburetors were revamped for increased fuel mileage and lowered emissions. The increase in displacement and new mixers yielded better performance and fuel mileage than the CB500 setup.

The bikes picked up a "K-year" designation in 1976, as did all of the other CB street bikes, and the 1977–78 models had new reverse-cone shaped mufflers, revised fuel tanks with safety lids, and turn signals mounted back with the taillight bracket. Honda carried the original

The "Sweet Sister" to the "Big Brother" CB750 Four, the CB500 Four was introduced in 1971 as a lighter, more agile, and lower-to-the-ground alternative to the CB750. For women and men of shorter stature, this was a dream come true. Top speed was about 110 miles per hour. *AMA*

CB-550

Metallic Brown

CB500-K0 design all the way to 1982 as the 63 horsepower CB650, continuously upgrading the top end over the same basic 11-year-old bottom-end design.

As a companion to the new CB750F and CB400F, the 1975 550s gained a new sports model, the CB550FK0 in 1975, which became the CB550F '76 and '77 in the following years. These came in candy and metal-flake orange and blue and red colors and were equipped with the new factory 4:1 exhaust system, with a large, cigar-shaped muffler. Mechanically, they were CB550Ks in sports clothing, though, and they achieved no great power gains.

Visually the same as the preceding CB500 Fours, the CB550 enjoyed a pleasing improvement to the powerband and performance thanks to the addition of the extra displacement and a new set of carburetors.

The 1976 CB550F ran concurrently with the CB400F and CB750F Super Sports models, as Honda began its serious focus into early "sport bike" models. It was available in blue, orange, or red.

In 1979, when the SOHC CB750s gave way to the new DOHC designs, Honda bored and stroked the 550 motors out to 627cc and called them CB650s. With suitable refinements to the rest of the engine components, the horsepower jumped to 63, and suddenly their milquetoast line of midrange machines was running 12-second quarter-miles! The first-generation machine featured Honda's new Comstar wheels, 4:2 mufflers, and electronic ignitions.

In 1980–81 the standard CB650s had reverted to wire wheels, while the Comstars were left on the new CB650C Custom series, with pulled-back bars, stepped seats, and four megaphone-shaped mufflers. The 1981 bikes received new air-adjustable forks and the Custom was graced with double disc brakes on the front. For 1982, which was the final year, Honda designated the bike the CB650SC '82 for the SC-series (Nighthawk). These models received a blacked-out engine treatment, new fuel tank/side covers, and a color-matched frame (blue or black).

The fourth and last year for the Super Sports models with factory four-into-one exhaust systems was 1978. *AMA*

Riding the Honda CB550-650 SOHC fours is the most natural thing a driver can imagine. They are much more user-friendly than CB750s for average-sized riders, and just about anyone could sit on any of these machines with comfort and confidence in traffic or on the highway. The suspensions are set on the comfy side, with the usual combination of too-soft front and too-firm rear springing. You can easily troll them around town from stoplight-to-stoplight without slipping the clutch or revving the engine a great deal. They are very docile and flexible in their demeanor and mechanically quiet. The original four-pipes have a pleasant and throaty sound when you get the revs up. The seats are certainly adequate for most short distance riding, and the overall handling of the chassis at speed inspires confidence and riding enjoyment. Only a crowded shift lever area, due to the proximity of the engine's left-side crankshaft-mounted generator, requires some adjustment for those with even averaged-sized feet.

The engines are easy to service, with angled valve cover caps allowing access to the screw-type adjusters. The ignition is located on the right end of the crankshaft with two sets of points and condensers mounted on the backing plate. The 500-650 fours are designed so that you can do a whole top-end overhaul without removing the engine. Once the carburetors are accurately set, they hold their synchronization for a long time.

The 1971–78 500-550s are just "above-average" performers, but their overall smoothness and rideability made them favorites for many riders in the 1970s. If you want a bike that is reliable, quiet, non-intimidating, then the 500-650s are worth a serious look.

CB350F (1973–74)

Machines even smaller than 500cc four-cylinders were introduced in 1973 in the form of the CB350 fours, equipped with a five-speed transmission and a 4:4 exhaust system, just like their bigger brothers. Smooth and sweet, they are at a disadvantage in the power-to-weight department but are well suited to riders who can't quite get comfortable with the CB500s. Honda offered them as an alternative to the buzzy CB350-360 twins during the time of the gas crisis, hoping to woo drivers out of their four-wheeled gas-guzzlers and onto something comfortable and economical. Honda geared up to meet an expected demand for fuel-efficient vehicles, but the U.S. public didn't believe that the gas crisis would be long-lived, and a glut of two-wheelers built up in many motorcycle warehouses in the mid-1970s. Much was written about this "baby four," but the bottom line was that the 350F's lack of power overshadowed its fine qualities. "Something nice for the girls to learn on" was the attitude about this machine. The CB350F has

How small can you go? Honda downsized the four-cylinder concept from 750 to 500 to 350 cc! These beautiful jewel-like machines copied their bigger brothers with four-into-four mufflers, four carbs, and smooth, quiet, watch-like motors. *AMA*

its share of supporters and restorers, but those cute little CB350F four separate mufflers are getting nearly impossible to find nowadays, and they cost more than $600, if you can find them. Thus, you should restore a CB350F only for love and not for money. Overall, the resale value of the CB400F to a CB350F is about 2-to-1 in favor of the cafe-styled machine.

CB400F (1975–77)

After two years of mediocre sales, the milquetoast CB350F was transformed into the handsome CB400F Super Sports model, which really came alive with the addition of 50cc and another gear in the transmission.

Gone were the fully enclosed front fork assemblies, now exposed with a dust cover at the top of the lower fork legs. Gone was the lightly sculpted "bread loaf" fuel tank, replaced with a smart-looking, softly angular rendition in blazing red or dark blue (a canary yellow color was added in 1976, replacing the dull blue), and gone were the riser handlebars, replaced with something that could have come from a flat-bar Super Hawk!

The stylish, comfortable 1975 CB400F is recognized as the "Sweetheart of the 1970s." With 37 horsepower, six speeds, factory four-into-one exhaust, sleek styling, and a solid powertrain, the CB400F gave many thrills to many riders, worldwide. Solid originals are always worth more than the 1975 asking price of $1,395. These became classics as soon as they were produced. *AMA*

The sleek 4:1 exhaust system echoes those found on the 1975 CB750F and CB550-F Super Sports models. If ever there was an "instant classic" design, this was it. The model was produced for a total of three years, the 1977 versions being somewhat emasculated with "western" handlebars replacing the low flat bars and more forward-mounted footpegs instead of the semirear set pegs of the original design. Nevertheless, the 1975–77 Honda CB400Fs are on the top of many collectors' lists. For a number of years, CB400Fs were returned back to Japan by the container-loads for a hungry home market, paying premium prices for bikes that normally sold for half that in the United States. The classic styling of the entire machine, especially the 4:1 exhaust, just seems to resonate with many, many Honda enthusiasts around the world.

At 408 pounds, Honda finally had answered the call and brought forth some worthy competition for the Yamaha RD 350-400s, the Kawasaki 250-350 Triples, and the Suzuki GT 380 Triples that were dominating the street and racing scenes. Here was an eye-catching, smooth, four-stroke four that had some performance to it and made a good racing platform for many would-be racers like myself.

The only problem with the bike was the noncompetitive power to weight ratio when compared to the screaming two-strokes. Hondas, being what they are, have large safety margins built into the engines and chassis, leaving room for improvements in performance without being fragile. Fortunately, a number of speed-equipment manufacturers saw the potential in this machine, and new "go-fast" items came to market quickly.

One of the most famous versions of the CB400F was built by Kaz Yoshima and unveiled by the then-editor of *Cycle News,* John Ulrich, at Ontario Motor Speedway. Built under Production Bike rules, it was a terror on the racetrack. The engine was bored to 458cc, and the heavily breathed-on motor would spin past 12,000, propelling the machine to 130-plus on the straightaways. Nimble and way under 400 pounds, it would wind its way through the turns with little effort and then burst through the gears again on the back straight. It won Open Production races, topping all comers in all displacements from 600cc and up. Both Kaz Yoshima and Pops Yoshimura offered high-performance engine parts for these engines, and the market was brisk with takers.

The cafe racer look was late arriving to the United States, so there was a lot of U.S. sales resistance to 400Fs at the time, due to their low handlebars fitted on the first two years. In 1977, Honda did a revamp in the ergonomics department. The new bikes were fitted with western riser handlebars, and the footpegs were brought forward a little. A new fuel tank featured similar overall styling but was given a new set of graphics and a flip-lid cover for the fuel filler neck. The new footpeg location allowed for a single-piece shift lever, replacing the former remote linkage system.

The change to "up" bars required a whole new set of cables, handlebar switches, and a new front brake hose to fit the increase in height. These changes made the bike a little less focused on the sport riders and more appealing to those who liked the bike but wanted to fit a windshield or some touring accessories. Having lost some of its original luster in the eyes

The graceful, sweeping turns of the factory four-into-one exhaust pipes on the CB400F were an eye-grabbing feature; however, to achieve the merging of pipes in this fashion, the exhaust pipes were of unequal length, thus limiting the top-end power potential of the engine. Just a change to an equal length system would add another 1,000 rpm to the power curve. All in all, the stock exhaust system was an integral part of the aesthetic balance of the machine and is a necessary part of any correct restoration.

of the purists, the new edition was left to languish along with the other leftover models until one of Honda's warehouse blowout sales. Still a fine machine, the 1977 models are less sought-after than the 1975–76 versions, owing to the emasculating changes made in the final year of production.

Finding original CB400Fs is getting increasingly difficult these days. The ones that have been stored need carburetor and brake caliper overhauls and usually a fresh set of fork seals. Partswise, Honda has supported the bikes more than others of their vintage, continuing to supply seat covers (one of the few models that had just the covers available), fuel tanks, side covers, and exhaust systems. With fluctuations in the yen to U.S. dollar, the prices have risen sharply for many replacement items. Fuel tanks alone are getting into the $300-plus price category. Still, there is an ongoing demand for the machines in the United States, and the appeal of this stylish and reliable machine will keep the prices high for years to come.

Chapter 7

The Modern Four-Cylinders

As soon as the other manufacturers got up to speed in competing with the SOHC Honda fours, Honda raised the ante by going to four-valve cylinder heads in its street bikes. Ironically, four-valve heads are what brought Honda so many world championships back in the 1960s. Honda timidly went back to its roots in 1973, with the four-valve, single-cam XL250 Motosports machine (followed by the XL350 in 1974), but the street bikes didn't see them until the CX500 V-twins were released in 1978. Three-valve heads did appear on the new CB/CM400T Hawks in that same year, however, so Honda was heading in the right direction.

Finally, in 1979, Honda brought out a whole new line of engines, based on four-valves-per-cylinder technology and DOHC. At the bottom end of the scale was the basic CB750K'79, and at the top was the muscular, inline, six-powered CBX. Horsepower figures jumped from the original SOHCs 67 to more than 80 in the new-series machines, and they were greeted with much enthusiasm in the press and by many Honda owners, who were probably beginning to shop around for something more current. The new bikes saved the day, and Honda race teams used them with great success on tracks around the world.

By 1983, though, the competition was relentlessly working on new, more advanced designs, so Honda responded in kind with a series of low-maintenance machines, using hydraulic lash adjusters. Hondas had always required regular valve adjustments, but the new 550-650-700 Nighthawk machines had done away with that requirement. Honda's philosophy has always been to make their products more powerful, easy, efficient, etc., and that is what they set about to do in each new project and product.

CB-1 (1989–90)

Part of Honda's late-1980s response to the dwindling number of "naked" entry-level bikes was to bring in the CB-1: a water-cooled, 400cc, 60-horsepower DOHC with gear-driven cams, 16 valves, and a six-speed gearbox. Although the CB-1 was quite popular in Japan in the late 1980s, it was not well received in the States. The CB-1 was a technological jewel, with 37-horsepower SOHC eight-valve motors, a sophisticated alloy frame, and disc brakes on both ends.

Unfortunately, Honda had priced the 1989 CB-1, Hawk GT650, and the GB500 within a few hundred dollars of each other; and that figure was way over what the market was used to paying for midsized

machinery, no matter what it looked like or how well it performed. Both bikes were sold only in 1989 and 1990 and then banished back to where they came from, where they continued to sell at a steady clip for some years after.

CB-1s have a redline at 13,000 rpm and highly tuned ones can pull up past 14,000 rpm. The engine is related to the CBR600 Hurricanes, sold as the original 600cc Sport Bike in the United States; in fact the CBR600 motor is a shoo-in for the CB-1 chassis, making it a serious hybrid canyon racer.

550–700cc Nighthawks (1983–91)

In 1983, new-design four-valve 550, 650, and 700cc engines with hydraulic lash adjusters made their way into CB550-650-700SC Nighthawk machines, all fitted with shaft-driven final drives and modern styling. The 1983–85 CB550-650SCs were custom-cruiser-styled, while the 700SC version had a quarter fairing and looked more like a sport bike than its smaller siblings. The basic design carried through into the 1991 standard CB750 Nighthawk, brought forth as a chain-drive machine, that is, smooth and extremely reliable. The 700SC continues to be highly regarded and sought after, with prices reaching $2,000. With the maintenance-free motor and shaft-drive, it is a terrific choice for sport-touring applications.

This 1979 CB750K Limited Edition commemorates the 10th anniversary of the release of the first CB750. Unlike the larger CB900–1000C machines, which featured shaft drive and a dual-range transmission, the CB750C still had a chain-driven rear wheel and five-speed gearbox. The stepped seat, pullback handlebars, Comstar wheels, and rear chromed fender were substantial upgrades from the wire-wheeled CB750K.

The new generation 550–650s, introduced in 1983, featured four-valve cylinder heads with hydraulic lash adjusters and shaft drives. *AMA*

750–1100cc Fours (1979–83)

A whole new series of 750-1047cc machines swept away the old SOHC designs in 1979. The new CB750K and a CB750K Limited Edition model held down the spot for the old-design machine. With four separate exhaust pipes, the standard K held over the wire wheel look, while the LTD (commemorating the tenth anniversary of the CB750) featured Comstar wheels, special paint, emblems, and mufflers. A new CB750F Sports model replaced the SOHC 750F machines and had a new 4:2 muffler system and quicker-steering chassis.

The new-design DOHC cylinder heads were air-cooled and had a four-valves-per-cylinder design, with the camshafts riding on "shims-on-top" valve buckets. High-output generators now had brushes, in automotive fashion, to help feed the new, much-brighter halogen headlights.

The DOHC lineup filled in with 750, 900, 1000, and 1100cc fours 1979 to 1983. The CB750-900F Super Sport bikes were noted for their fine handling and solid reliability, although some engines of this series had link-plate cam chain failures. The most collectible of the DOHC Super Sports models, besides the CBX, is the CB1100F, which was only sold in 1983. This bike incorporates the benefits of the CB750-900F chassis with a big-bore top end and antidive, air-adjustable front forks. It also featured a factory 1/4 fairing and cast wheels in place of the previous Comstar wheels fitted to most of the big Honda street bikes from 1978 to 1982.

The Nighthawk S, with its shaft drive and hydraulic valve lash adjusters, was the ultimate low-maintenance sports machine. A stylish quarter-fairing, TRAC antidive fork, double disc brakes up front, and a six-speed transmission rounded out the factory installed features.

Honda's other variation on a theme was the CB900-1000 Custom series, which featured shaft-drive and a dual-range five-speed gearbox, effectively yielding 10 forward speeds. The 900s were sold from 1980 to 1982, with the 1000 version offered only in 1983. This is another one of Honda's "one-off" models from that year, including the reworked CX/GL650s, which were superseded by all-new machinery in 1984. How amazing that Honda would go to the expense of retooling a machine for only one season! It is hard to imagine the size and scope of Honda's engineering department, which is able to work on so many models simultaneously, and still have them all turn out so well.

The 1983 CB1100F was the largest and most powerful of the double overhead cam fours, but was offered for only a single year. Unique features were the quarter fairing with rectangular headlight, TRAC antidive fork, and cast-alloy wheels. *Fred Hunter collection*

Chapter 8

The CBX and the Gold Wing

Honda's history with six-cylinder machines dates back to the 1960s when its howling Grand Prix racers were engineering marvels that dominated the senses with their sound and won championships with performance. The sixes in question here are the legendary CBX and the venerable Gold Wing (which eventually became a six-cylinder). The CBX set the world on fire with horsepower, sound, and a style dominated by a wide, menacing inline six-cylinder engine. The Gold Wing transformed the industry as well, perhaps to a larger degree, but in a much less dramatic fashion. The Wing's flat-four brought civilized, reliable power to a bike designed for the road. Wings are not considered highly collectible as of yet, but the early ones have become sought after by those whose early days of touring began on the original GL1000.

Honda stepped into the "big bike" market with the 1975 GL1000 Gold Wing and nursed that machine along, refining and revising it as the marketplace requested. Adding the six-cylinder CBX to the lineup really made a statement to the competition about what Honda could do with its engineering expertise. As Harley-Davidson's fortunes continued to rise, it was obvious that there was a solid market for touring and one-liter-sports machines.

When Honda finally added its full-dress versions of the Gold Wing to the lineup, its own fortunes took an upturn. These machines would leave the H-D dressers in the dust in almost all categories. While Honda's reputation was well established for the touring set, the battle for supremacy on the streets and racetracks was far from resolved. The release of the complex and powerful CBX left many questions unanswered about Honda's intentions in that market segment. Although the CB1100F was to be Honda's remaining one-liter class performance flagship after the CBX's transformation into Sports Tourer, there wouldn't be another machine quite like the CBX until the CBR1100XX Black Bird was released in 1997 as the new-generation king-of-the-hill horsepower champion (where the crown usually lasts for only about a year before being toppled). Honda's ultimate replacement for the 1981–82 CBX Sports Touring bike didn't come until about 10 years later, in the form of the muscular ST1100: a transverse, V-4 powered machine.

As far as a pure one-liter sports machine goes, the 1993 CBR900RR was the next dedicated, large-displacement machine to put Honda back on the racetrack in its customary first position. It's possible that the CBX was just Honda flexing its engineering muscles, proving once again that it could produce whatever it wanted, be it small or large. Engineering pride has been the corner-stone of Honda's sales and racing successes for over 50 years.

To this day, some 22 years after their introduction, the CBXs continue to turn heads wherever they go. The CBX owner's club has been in existence for almost as long as the bike has been on the market, and clubs like this continue to offer parts and service support for this classic machine. Despite the apparent complexity, once a CBX is "dialed-in,"

it is very reliable and long-lived. The CBX, in all forms, is a shining example of Honda's legacy of imagination and innovation.

CBX (1979–82)

In 1979 horsepower was the name of the game, and for a brief time, the CBX was the king of the hill. Despite the power of the impressive six-banger, the chassis was not up to the task of spirited riding. Desperate attempts to keep the weight below 600 pounds showed up in undersized fork diameters coupled with flexing frames and swing arms. The 1980 edition saw some improvements in the chassis, with a needle-bearing swingarm pivot of increased size and slightly wider rims and tires, but the single-piston brakes were still not up to the task of hauling the big machine down from high speeds quickly and repeatedly.

Through the clever use of "jackshafts" running off of the crankshaft, the width of a CBX six was a scant couple of inches wider than a CB750 motor at the bottom. The intake camshaft was driven off of the center of the crankshaft, but the exhaust cam ran off of a tandem intake cam sprocket with its own horizontal tensioner. The 24 valves had adjustment shims that rested on top of the valve spring buckets for easier maintenance. Because the CBX had a shorter stroke than the companion DOHC fours, it had a higher redline.

Ignition was breakerless, using three double-ended coils and three separate solid-state igniters. The six separate carburetors were all ganged together on a rack, to be installed as a single unit. Final drive was through a massive 630 chain in 1979, but this was changed over to a 530 pitch in 1980.

Honda abandoned the idea of the CBX as a Super Bike and reconfigured it as a Sport Tourer in 1981–82, finally fitting it with larger forks, ventilated front brake rotors with twin-piston calipers, as well as a version of the single-shock Pro-Link rear suspension, as featured on the dirt bikes.

The 1979 CBX was the first production double overhead cam, 24-valve inline-six-cylinder bike for the street. With 103 horsepower, it was the "King of the Hill" for that year. It was one of Honda's wildest street machines ever, but unsuitable for road racing. Big-bore kits and turbocharging made it competitive at the drags, though. The next year saw some chassis upgrades and a little detuning to drop the power output below the 100-horsepower level required in the German market. *AMA*

Detuned for more midrange power and 75 pounds heavier, these bikes were slow sellers at the $5,595 price, and many were donated to auto/motorcycle shops at high schools, colleges, and in some cases, prison rehabilitation programs by American Honda.

CBX (1980)

The 1980 model CBX came with the dreaded vacuum-operated petcock fuel system (a good idea, but poorly executed). There were upgrades to the chassis from the original design, which were welcome improvements, but most CBX owners are aware of the difficulty of getting their 1980 model bikes started after they've been sitting for more than a few days. Even a little fuel evaporation from the float bowls will cause the bikes to starve before the petcock can replenish the supply to half a dozen hungry carburetors during the startup drill. Continuous cranking of the starter motor only drains the battery and overheats the starter motor and electrical circuits. CBX owners have created a number of fixes and bypasses, and this information is available through organizations like the International CBX Owner's Club. Despite some detuning to get the engine output below 100 horsepower, the overall improvements to the 1980 versions were mostly positive. The 1980 bikes were assembled in the new Marysville, Ohio, plant and some 7,500 were rolled out the door that year.

CBX Sport Kits

The first step for many U.S. CBX riders was to order and install the CBX Sport Kit, which consists of lower European handlebars and more rearward positioned footpegs. This comprehensive kit includes all of the cables, hoses, wires, and switches needed to make a complete conversion.

Replacing the throttle cables during the Sport Kit installation requires removing the exhaust and lowering the engine in the chassis to access the cables and/or remove the rack of carburetors. Stock CBXs have a lean spot off-idle, so owners often switch to one step richer main and pilot jets while they have the carbs off. These bikes' high-speed stability can be upset by the addition of bodywork or sometimes just a change in the mirrors, so one must proceed with caution when installing nonapproved, aftermarket accessories. CBXs with handlebar-mounted fairings are prone to begin a speed wobble over 100 miles per hour, so be careful.

Riding a CBX

Just as your whole sense of what a motorcycle was changed after your first experience with a CB750 in 1969, the sensory inputs of a six-cylinder, 105 horsepower, CBX take your frame of reference to even greater heights.

At 600 pounds it was certainly the biggest bike in Honda's lineup, other than a Gold Wing. The first ride reveals that accelerating through first and second gears, at redline, yields 80 miles per hour, with three gears to go. One of just my favorite motorcycle experiences is running any CBX through the first two gears at 10,000 rpm—a thrilling symphony of sound and motion.

Honda's last gasp at salvaging something good from the CBX-motored machines was to completely redesign the bikes for 1981, giving them a new chassis with Pro-Link rear suspension, new larger forks, double piston brakes with ventilated rotors, and full sport touring bodywork. The conversion added 75 more pounds to the original design, and midrange punch was increased at the expense of the top-end rush. Silver in 1981, they were painted a beautiful Pearl White in 1982 and then they were gone. *AMA*

CBX Sport Touring (1981–82)

If you ride the 1981–82 Sport Touring versions of the bike, you will appreciate the amount of engineering design that went into the second generation edition, including more appropriately sized forks; vented brake rotors, now grabbed by twin piston brake calipers; Pro-Link single shock rear suspension and a more luxurious seat; and of course, the full bodywork package. Unfortunately, it was a lot of work for little reward at the showrooms, and the later models never found the following of the original Super Bike designs.

CBX Reliability

Overall, despite the apparent complexity of the CBXs, maintaining them is pretty easy and straightforward. The rack of six carburetors holds its synchronization well; the ignition is electronic; the valves seldom need adjusting after the first 10,000 miles; and they can easily run 50,000 miles on the original top ends.

The only serious problem was with the early models, when the bikes were left on the side stands and the petcock was left on for a while. If one of the carburetor needles leaked and overflowed, the ganged-together bowl vent tubes would collect all of the raw fuel and deposit it in the number one cylinder. If the valves happened to be open, the cylinder would fill with gasoline, which is a noncompressible liquid. The next time you fired up the bike, the number one rod would bend, trying to do the impossible task of squeezing liquid gasoline into a fraction of its previous volume. This is damaging and requires a costly repair, and it probably caused the creation of the 1980 model's vacuum petcock, which does not flow fuel until the engine is running. Had Honda used a "prime" position on its petcock, like that on some of the other brands, the problem would not be so great. Of course, if you left the petcock on prime and parked it on the side stand, you would be back to square one! On the early models, you can help prevent the problem by using individual bowl lines rather than the collected set that came from the factory.

The CBX is sought by Honda collectors. The bikes are not that hard to find, as 21,000 of them were sold in 1979. Again, if you are restoring one, the exhaust system will be expensive and hard-to-find. A complete system could easily cost over $800. A number of aftermarket systems are still available, though, if you just want to ride your machine and enjoy the delightful experience of those six busy pistons making beautiful music wherever you go.

Gold Wing (1975–2000)

Certainly no reference to Honda products can be complete without mentioning the bike that started its own market: the GL1000 Gold Wing. Whole books have been written about Wings, and they spawned a new lifestyle in motorcycling.

The 75 GL1000 Gold Wing launched Honda into the touring bike market, even though it came "naked" from the factory. This was the first Honda motorcycle to use a driveshaft, belt-driven cams, and watercooling. Even at 600 pounds, the power is there to send it down the road at over 125 miles per hour, with all the smoothness of an Accord. *AMA*

In 1976, Honda offered both a standard Gold Wing model in red or yellow, plus a Limited Edition in Candy Brown in 1976. The wheels/spokes and all of the emblems and striping on the LTD were gold. The radiator shroud was chrome-plated and a special leather tool kit bag was included.

The last year you could buy a "naked" version of a Gold Wing was 1984.

First-year editions are still quite collectible bikes, with an 85-horsepower flat-four breathing through a quartet of big CV carburetors, a very fast and big machine for its day. Road tests indicated a good 125 miles per hour top speed. With a silky-smooth powerplant and a shaft-drive handling the five speeds coming from the rugged transmission, this bike was built to cruise the highways in comfort and quiet. Why Honda waited until 1980 to wrap these water-cooled smoothies in their own bodywork one can only guess. Surely, Craig Vetter and his fellow aftermarket accessory company buddies can do nothing but praise the creation of those early Gold Wings.

The original 1000cc machine changed very little in the first four years of the model. A Limited Edition package was available for 1976 models. The package added gold-trimmed rims and emblems and a special seat. Comstar wheels were added in 1978.

In 1980 the engine was punched out a bit and the model became the GL1100. That bike turned a respectable 12.47-second 107-miles per hour quarter-mile time in a *Cycle* magazine test. The GL1100I Interstate was added to the line, a bike which had factory bags and a fairing. This was the model that began the Wing's transformation from a big, powerful, naked bike well suited to traveling into an electronically equipped touring machine.

GOLD WING™ INTERSTATE™

The Interstate was the stripped-down touring version of the Gold Wing, and in 1985 the least expensive version, as Honda did not offer a standard version that year.

The Aspencade, named for a famous touring rally, featured a host of luxury features, such as an on-board air compressor and a built-in stereo system.

In 1982 the addition of the GL1100A Aspencade took the Wing a step closer toward its present incarnation, adding an onboard compressor that offered on the fly suspension adjustments and an upgraded audio system. All of the 1982 Wings received dual-piston front brakes and self-canceling turn signals as well.

In 1984 engine displacement was bumped to 1182cc and the Wing became the GL1200. Over the ensuing four model years, the Wing received improved electronics, audio systems, and so on. In the process, the bike created its own motorcycling niche.

In 1988 the model was totally revised, with a 1520cc opposed six-cylinder engine and a new look that was more Accord than it was GL. Since that time, the Wing has become the most refined and popular bike in its class. Even today, the Gold Wing is still king.

GOLD WING™ ASPENCADE™

Honda's 1985 Limited Edition Gold Wing was Honda's first nonturbocharged fuel-injected motorcycle. This version weighed 41 pounds more than the Aspencade and had special paint, graphics, and trim pieces. In 1986 a similar fuel-injected version, the Aspencade SE-I, featured a special ivory/beige metallic paint and graphics combination.

GOLD WING™ LIMITED EDITION

The Sporting V-Fours (1983–2000)

Honda's V-4 sportbike legacy was fueled by racing. Never one to shy away from a challenge, Honda often approached racing as a do-or-die proposition, pouring money into research, development, and top-class talent. The combination was hard to beat, and it also led to the development of the V-4 engine for competition.

By developing four-stroke V-4 engines for Grand Prix racing, Honda got a taste of what this technology could do. They were not always successful on the GP front, but the technology they developed made its way to the street when the V45 Sabre and Magna were introduced in 1982. That delightful V-4 engine was then used as a basis to create the 1983 Interceptor. The VF750F Interceptor was sleek, technologically amazing, and styled more radically than anything else in the class. Backed by a monstrous factory budget, Honda went after the Superbike title with a vengance. Although Eddie Lawson and Kawasaki won the title that year,

Honda's factory-backed 750 Interceptors reigned supreme in the mid-1980s. Horsepower was up from the street version's 86 to the low 100s. Freddie Spencer and Mike Baldwin had great success with these bikes. *AMA*

In 1984, Honda downsized the V45 Sabre to 698 cc, versus the original 750-cc displacement of the 1982–1983 models.

The 1983 750 Interceptor was a blockbuster, not unlike the original CB750. Honda scrapped the inline-4 design for a compact, water-cooled V-4 in order to compete with other manufacturers in the AMA 750 Superbike series. The 750 Interceptor was rated at 86 horsepower, had a six-speed transmission, and featured a 16-inch front wheel. The alloy perimeter chassis was an all-new design. Honda had success immediately, especially at the hands of Freddie Spencer and his team, and demand for the street version was very strong. Other than some new graphics, there was little to change in the 1984 version shown.

The Magnas were Honda's most popular V-4s in the early 1980s. The 700-cc version shown here was built in response to the tariff on imported bikes over 700-cc imposed by the U.S. government in 1984.

Honda took the "custom" concept to a new level with the Magna series, especially with the V65 versions. These bikes were fully equipped to MOVE down the highway! A water-cooled, 121-horsepower, four-valve, V-4 engine was coupled to a six-speed transmission, which fed those power pulses through a driveshaft to the rear wheel. An integral fiber-optic antitheft system was standard equipment, along with triple-disc brakes to bring it all to a halt.

Honda's V-4s were a crucial part of the creation of another new category of motorcycles, the sportbike.

The V-4 made its way into several incarnations of the sportbike, evolving from high-tech sportbikes into refined sporting machines designed for high-performance street use, as seen in the VFR800.

VF750/700F (1983–85)

The 1983 Interceptor features an 86-horsepower engine in an all-new perimeter frame, with a 16-inch front wheel, antidive forks, and twin-piston brakes. The narrow powerplant made good power but was still top-heavy and not a great deal lighter than the bike it had replaced. Not long after the V-4s hit the streets, it became evident that an oiling problem was damaging camshafts, followers, and cylinder heads (as the cams ran directly on the machined head surfaces). With the number of components in the top end, the repairs were very costly. Honda recalled and redesigned several components in order to cure this tendency toward self-destruction. A number of aftermarket companies offer oiling kits that greatly enhance the Interceptor's longevity.

Honda repackaged the delightful 500-cc V-4 engine in a "Magna" series chassis and bodywork, and named it the V30 Magna.

The sixth gear on a V65 was an overdrive, allowing for a very relaxed engine at highway speeds. If they could have achieved their powerpeak in top gear, top speed would have been about 170 miles per hour! Even so, they would pull over 140 in fifth, which is good considering the lack of aerodynamics and the sit-up riding position.

With the addition of Honda's Hondaline touring accessories, an owner could transform his or her V65 Sabre into a fast and stylish sport-tourer, a role in which the large bike excelled. *Bob Hampton collection*

While the race bikes were doing well in competition, there were a lot of complaints about the tendency of the bikes to "stand up" in corners with the brakes applied due to the 16-inch front wheel, and getting proper tires was a problem because Honda was one of the few manufacturers specifying this size wheel. Most tire manufactures were reluctant to spend a lot of development and tooling money on such a limited application.

VF500F (1984–86)

One year after the V45 Interceptor was introduced, the baby brother VF500F hit dealer floors. Perhaps the best of the original Interceptors, the 68-horsepower VF500F combined smooth,

One of the most balanced V-4 packages from Honda was the 500-cc Interceptor. It has a nearly vibration-free, 60-plus horsepower engine coupled with a slick-shifting six-speed transmission, PRO-LINK rear suspension, TRAC antidive front fork, and triple disc brakes. The short wheelbase and centralized powerplant mass leads to quick, nimble steering on and off the racetrack, making for great fun in a small package. *AMA*

torquey power with a light, nimble chassis. One of the easiest bikes to ride fast at that time, the Interceptor's baby brother remains a great little bike. The bike received a makeover in 1986, with bolder red, white, and blue graphics, black wheels, red fork legs, and a red seat.

VFR750/700 (1986–87)

In 1986, Honda made a quantum leap in upgrading the V-4s. By redesigning the entire engine into a gear-drive system for the cams, Honda pretty much eliminated the cam wear gremlins. The first series of these bikes, in the federally mandated 700 size and the full 750cc flavor, ran for 24 hours at a Texas track and set new average speed records of over 140 miles per hour.

The 750s were red, white, and blue both years, while the tariff-ducking 700s could be had in pearl white or red, white, and blue in 1986 and a handsome dark blue or pearl white in 1987. Both the 750s and the 700s made electric-smooth power, with a combination of reasonable low-end torque, decent midrange, great top-end power, and the distinctive V-4 howl. The suspension on the 1986 version, however, left something to be desired. An aftermarket shock and a stiffer set of fork springs help significantly. Grafting early CBR600 front forks stiffens things up considerably as well, but requires some machining to make it work.

The tariff-beating 700-cc version of the gear-driven-cam F2 version of the Interceptor was down 5 horsepower from the full 750-cc models. The 1987 models were essentially the same as the 1986s, except for cosmetic changes and a new digital ignition system. *AMA*

VFR750/800 (1990–2000)

While the VFR lived on in Europe, the model was not brought into the United States until 1990, when another new generation of the bike appeared. The bike featured a single-sided swingarm and sexy red paint in a package that had given up a titch of sporting edge in favor of day-to-day usability. Ensuing incarnations of this generation VFR750 had a black paint job and the less-popular refrigerator white machine.

The VFR was redesigned in 1994, with a smaller, slightly softly sprung chassis, a more modern look, and a slightly lower-revving, midrange-oriented motor. These bikes were in production through 1997, garnering praise from magazines and enthusiasts as the sport-touring motorcycle of choice.

In 1998 the VFR800FI replaced the 750, featuring a bit more displacement, fuel injection, a heavily refined design that dropped the weight and tightened the dimensions, an improved version of Honda's linked braking system, and a styling makeover. The new engine made power reminiscent of the 1986–87 VFRs, with a slightly soft but usable low-end, strong hit in the midrange, and solid top-end power. Combined with stiffer suspension settings and a very solid, slightly smaller chassis, the new 800 added some more sport to the VFR, while roomier ergonomics and a new seat retained the bike's all-day riding comfort. The bike remained relatively unchanged and Honda-red until 2000, when a yellow version was offered.

Brute size kept the VF1000F Interceptor, offered only in 1984, from being a sales success. It is rare to find these bikes in original condition anymore.

VF1000F/1000R (1984–86)

The heavy, chain-driven VF1000F and gear-driven VF1000R Interceptor machines have gone into the archives of motorcycle history as memorable, but not highly desirable, machines. The F is probably the better motorcycle to ride on the street, but the R's gear-drive and racer-boy graphics have more appeal to the collector.

RC-30 (1989–90)

The limited-production RC-30s (VFR750R) were handmade street bikes, based on the factory road racers, featuring such goodies as titanium connecting rods, a six-speed close-ratio gearbox, hand-laid fiberglass bodywork, and myriad exquisitely executed details. At $14,995, they were far and away the most expensive street bikes sold in the United States at that time. Fine examples are still fetching five figures. They are truly works of art, in motion or just parked in the garage.

Ever since the introduction of the VF750F Interceptor sports machine, Honda has had a strong following with the concept and the continuously upgraded versions of the 750 V-4-series machines. When Honda wanted to continue to upgrade and compete with the VFR750 machines in both AMA and World Super bike racing, it had to offer the street versions of its racing bikes to the general public.

Magazine testers were quick to put the exotic RC-30 through its paces in order to justify or disprove to their readers the wisdom of investing such a sum into a limited production street bike. The RC-30 was the first production street bike to come fitted with titanium connecting rods from the factory. The feathery machine weighed in at just over 400 pounds and the horsepower was claimed to be about 100. Because of its close relationship to its roadracing brethren, the RC-30 had a close-ratio gearbox more suited to Daytona than to the street. Thus, the quarter-mile times were substandard, even for the standard VFR750 street bikes. The testing did reveal an almost intuitive level of steering control and suspension manners, once the multisetting suspenders were adjusted to suit the rider.

The VF1000R was made only in 1985–1986 model years. The heavy and complex 1,000-cc V-4 features gear-driven cams and 150-mile per hour top speeds. *AMA*

The seductive bodywork is all hand-laid fiberglass and the fit and finish were nothing short of Honda's best for a street bike. RC-30s were snapped up as collector's items right out of the box, and more than a few were left in the box for safekeeping. Many others were placed into racing service, however, and others were modified to suit the owners' tastes. Truly a classic right from the beginning, the RC-30 still draws a crowd whenever it makes an appearance. With its limited distribution, spare parts are rare and quite costly. When the bike was introduced, the rear cowling assembly behind the seat cost about $2,000 alone, so if you buy one, don't drop it!

The RC-30 continues to be available in original condition from those who trade in it as a commodity rather than a tool for the street, but even ten years later, the prices are often in the five-digit range. Still, for the money, you get a tremendous piece of motorcycle history, and you will belong to an exclusive club of owners. For reference, when the fuel-injected RC-45s came out about 5 years later, they listed at $25,000, so a fine RC-30 is a bargain at half or less that price! Honda has claimed many race wins and championships with the RC30 since its introduction. Owning the street version honors the rich tradition and heritage of this outstanding racing machine from Honda's engineering team.

Honda's V-4 sportbikes are unique, desirable machines. While only a few of these bikes are collectible today—notably the RCs and perhaps first- and second-generation VF/VFRs—these are bikes that will most likely maintain value for some time. More importantly, these machines are high-quality, reliable, functional machines that are simply great bikes to ride.

Only 300 RC30s were sold in the United States in 1990, at $14,995 each. Basically street versions of the factory 750-cc road racers, they were the first street bikes sold with titanium connecting rods. In order for Honda to race RC30s in the United States, they had to sell street-legal versions of the bikes. *AMA*

Chapter 10

Dual-Purpose, Mini-Trails, and Dirt Bikes

How many of us remember our first experience riding a Honda (or any other) motorcycle? It was probably on the dirt, wasn't it? If you are going to fall down while learning, then the dirt is the place to do it.

Honda's earliest attempts at racing its machines came at hillclimbs and scrambles races on unpaved race courses. As soon as Honda had its street bike lineup solidified, it went to work developing dual-purpose dirt bikes. Its first effort was the CL72, but a CL72 is an adult-sized machine, and kids don't want to wait until they can "reach the pedals" to enjoy the experience of motorcycle riding. Honda needed to make smaller machines so children could learn the basics of motorcycle operation.

Did you learn to ride motorcycles on a Mini-Trail?

With that purpose in mind, Honda released the CZ100 Monkey bike in the early 1960s, which came to the United States in late 1968 in the updated form of a Honda Z50 Mini-Trail. Cheap to buy and operate, it was close to the ground so the damage from the inevitable falls was lessened. Honda's focus on young riders grew as the kids grew up; Mini-Trails grew into CT70s, SL70s, and XR75s over the years.

In the late 1960s and early 1970s, as young teenagers outgrew the 50-70cc Mini-Trails, they had nothing to turn to in the Honda lineup. Many former Honda riders wound up on Yamaha 125-360cc Enduros, Kawasaki 100-350cc, or Suzuki 90-250cc two-stroke machines in order to quench their thirst for speed and thrills. The sport of off-road riding and motocross or scrambles racing was really taking off, and Honda had little to offer those riders.

That all changed with the introduction of the purpose-built CR250M Elsinore (and a year later the CR125M Elsinore) motocrossers. These were not little trail-bike toys! The last time Honda put the letters CR in front of a motorcycle model's name, it was building 12,000 rpm road racers. Honda was serious about the Elsinores, and the result was a streak of wins in both classes, including National Championships. Honda

Honda went two-stroke in 1973 with the blockbuster 248-cc CR-250 Elsinore motocross machine, weighing in at 214 pounds dry. *Bill Orazio*

The first Honda Z50K0 "Mini-Trails" were sent to the United States in 1969 without any lighting, as stripped-down learner machines for the kids. Subsequent K1 versions had battery-powered lighting and a horn, making them fully street-legal in many states. With full USDA-approved mufflers, they could be taken to campgrounds and used as grocery-getters for adventurous campers. With fold-down handlebars and sealable fuel systems, they could be safely stored in the trunk of a family sedan or station wagon. Mini-Trails are hot property these days, and restored versions are valued at over $2,500. *AMA*

softened up the basic models somewhat with some MT/MR125-175-250 woods and street-legal machines for a couple of years, but there would be no turning back for their motocross racing teams.

In addition to motocross action, Honda also set its sights on the Enduro and Desert racing scenes and released the XL250-350 series singles and a host of 100-125-175-185-200cc dual-purpose singles that were quite at home in the dirt and sand. Eventually the product line included XL/XR500s, which grew into the 500-650 models and are still with us in the new millennium.

Z-50 (1968–88)

If Honda 50cc Cubs put America's teenagers on two wheels in the early-to-mid-1960s, the Z-50 Mini-Trails put them on two wheels almost as soon as they could walk. Honda's original design minibike was the CZ100 Monkey bike, dating from 1964, but it never sold in the United States. This bike was an adaptation of the 4.3 horsepower (at 9,500 rpm) C100 three-speed auto-clutch engine, mated to a rigid frame. The tank and seat were borrowed from a domestic C111 Sports Cub and the handlebars were fixed in place. Weighing in at around 100 pounds, it carried front and rear lights and a horn, making it road-worthy.

The next generation, the Z50M, was also not imported into the United States. The 1967 Z50M featured the new OHC engine, detuned to 2.5 horsepower at 6,000 rpm. The convenience features of the new model included folding handlebars and an adjustable-height covered seat. This model was the forerunner to the first U.S.-version Z50A Mini-Trail 50 (Z50AK0), released in September of 1968. The Z50AKO came in either a candy red or bright yellow and silver color combination. The first releases were intended for child's play, in off-road situations, as they had no lights front or rear. The chassis was still a "hard tail" at the rear, but some rudimentary, undamped spring forks were fitted up front. Rear suspension did not arrive until the K3 versions in 1972.

When the K1s were released in March 1969, they were equipped with a battery to power front and rear lights, giving them full street-legal status in most states. The K2s were basically the same as the K0s and K1s, with the exception of some detail changes to the fuel tank emblems, control levers, and an extended rear fender.

When the 1972 Z50K3 Mini-Trail 50 adopted a newly designed frame with dual rear shocks, the tiny tank badges were replaced with decals, which came in different designs and colors over the years. The series continued, unchanged for the most part (other than graphics and cosmetic touches) until the last version: the Z50A 1978. After that, they went back to basics as off-road machines, without lights, as the Z50R 1979–88 models; but then the lights came back on again with the introduction of the all-new, perimeter-framed, single rear shock ZB50 1988, a one-year edition machine. Collectors snapped up the 20-year anniversary edition Z50RD 1986, which was an all-chromed model, harking back to some of Honda's all-chrome 50-90-305cc machines built in the early 1960s, as special appreciation gifts for the burgeoning American-market dealerships.

Z50s continued small evolutionary steps as the sales rose. Most of the changes were cosmetic up to this 1970 Z50K2, but the K3 bikes introduced in 1972 received some rear shocks to cushion a few of the bumps transmitted through the hardtail frames of the first series models. *AMA*

117

There wasn't much damping there, but from the K3 versions onward, there were shocks at the rear end of all Z50s.

QA50 (1970–75)

Introduced just after the Z50s, the QA50 was a dirt-only model for the tiny tikes, featuring a modest-output, pushrod, 50cc, two-speed, auto-clutch powerplant. Wheel rims were a scant 5 inches across, with their 4.00x5-inch knobby tires, partially encased by rugged, plastic fenders. Like little two-wheeled popsicles, they were adorned in colorful yellow, green, red, orange, and blue paint schemes and graphics, so parents could keep track of them in the not-too-far distance of the backyard. Fledgling riders could buzz around for hours on a tiny tank of gasoline, gaining confidence and riding skills, which were constantly challenged by the rigid-frame and short-travel, undamped spring forks. From here, the next step up was an MR50, once they were released in 1974. Unlike the Z50s, they never grew up to have aspirations as street-legal machinery and stayed pretty much in their original form for the full run of production in the first half of the 1970s; their tiny dimensions precluded most adults from commandeering them as pit bikes and motor home grocery-getters.

The QA50 was a tiny starter bike for the little ones. These four-stroke, two-speed machines came in bright kid's colors and could circle around the back forty for hours at a time while young riders developed their cycling skills.

118

CT70 (1969–82) and CT70H (1970–73)

About a year after the release of the Z50A in the fall of 1969, Honda brought out its bigger brother: the CT70K0, also known as the Mini-Trail 70. These came out as fully street-legal machines, including speedometers, battery, and full lighting. They were based on a simple but strong T-bone–shaped frame, with the fuel tank as a separate plastic container inside the frame. A 72cc version of the Z50 engine was installed along with the similar three-speed auto-clutch transmission.

In mid-1970, a special four-speed manual clutch version was added to the line, known as the CT70HK0, but this variation lasted only through to the following year's K1 edition, and then was dropped from the lineup. From the K1 models forward, the CT70s featured a separate speedometer instead of the usual speedo-in-a-headlight case, seen in many of that era's S90 and CT90 models. Like the Z50-series, they all had folding handlebars and sealable fuel systems that allowed them to be stowed horizontally in an automobile trunk without spilling gasoline inside the vehicle.

A member of the long-running series of favorite bikes for growing kids and thousands of motorhome owners, this 1970 CT70K0 is shown in a factory Honda photo. *Bill Orazio*

Despite many changes in graphics, muffler heat shields, turn signals, and seats, the bikes were primarily unchanged through the final series machine, the CT70 1982. But you can't keep a good bike down, and nine years later, the CT70 1991 came back to the dealerships for a four-year stint through 1994. The "new" models returned with the speedometers located back in the headlight shell again!

ST90 Trailsport 90 (1973–75)

The unique Trailsport model lasted only three years in the United States, from 1973 through 1975. Basically a more adult version of the CT70 Mini-Trails, they featured a similar T-bone frame with a three-speed auto-clutch transmission attached to an OHC 89cc engine. As with the other Mini-Trail siblings, the ST90 has quick release handlebars, which facilitate storage in the back of a automobile or van. Equipped with a full complement of battery-powered lights, horn, and turn signals, they are a compromise between the CT70 Mini-Trail and the more full-sized CT90 Trail 90. This street-legal package was the best of both worlds for many camping applications.

For those who had outgrown the CT70s and still wanted compact transportation for the motorhome or plane, the OHC ST90 was available for a three-year run. Auto clutch and full lighting made them completely street legal and easy to ride. *Bill Orazio*

SL70 (1971-73) & XL70 (1974-76)

As an addition to the SL Motosports lineup, Honda transplanted the CT70H motor into a new tube frame, added larger wire-spoke wheels, and created a new SL70K0-K1 machine. Light and nimble with actual hydraulic front forks, it was a perfect match to the larger 100/125/175/350 Motosports versions. In 1974 the Motosports moniker was dropped, and the whole range of machines was renamed XL, in this case XL70K0 through XL70 1976, carrying over the almost horizontal engine. In 1973 a whole new machine was redesigned, including the engine (75cc cylinder, now almost vertical, as the XR75), and was progressively expanded to 80cc (XR80 '79) and then to 100cc (1979 XL100S '79) configurations.

The XL70 line replaced the earlier SL70s in name, but not in form. The tiny, 72-cc horizontal cylinders and four-speed transmissions were used on both versions. For one year only (1976), Honda offered a green XL70 model. This was also the last before the changeover to the new XL75.

XL250-350 (1972–75)

Honda was incredibly busy in the early 1970s, with both new two-stroke Motocrossers and the launch of new four-stroke enduro bikes, dubbed Motosports. In 1973 alone, Honda offered 16 different road bikes, four dirt bikes, six on/off road bikes, and six more trail bikes, covering the entire spectrum from the 50cc QA50 to the mighty CB750, which sold 60,000 units that year. Prior to the 1972 introduction of the XL250K0 Motosport 250, the only pseudo-dirt bikes in the 250-350cc range were the grossly overweight SL350s, which still wore their electric starters until the 1970 K1s were released! Not that they were taken seriously as a true off-road machine anyway, but Honda really had no answer for the popular Yamaha DT/RT-series Enduros, which covered the span of 125 to 360cc, and challenging a 360cc RT-1 with an SL350 was an exercise in futility.

So right before the release of the CR250s, Honda sprung another surprise with the introduction of the new purpose-built XL250 Motosport 250, in the spring of 1972. From the ground up, this was a new design with a 22-horsepower, four-valve, four-stroke single, with a 2.75 x 21-inch front wheel, and tucked-in high exhaust on the left side. It weighed in at about 280 pounds. This marked Honda's first production engine with four-valves-per cylinder, as well as the first use of magnesium in some of its engine castings.

The engine was hugely over-square at 74 x 57.8 milllimeters and featured an angled intake port to accommodate the tucked-in rubber-mounted carburetor.

The first edition of the SL350, introduced in 1969, was more CB than SL, with an electric starter, CV carbs, and high revving engine. *Bill Orazio*

In 1972, Honda introduced its first production four-valve-per-cylinder engine, with the XL250. This 1974 model came with some modifications to muffler heat shields and a new paint scheme, but was primarily unchanged from the original version. *Bill Orazio*

Compression was set at 9:1 and power peaked at 8,000 rpm, with the torque cresting at 6,500 rpm. The engine and the bike, in general, stayed unchanged except for cosmetic updates until the XL250 '76 model, which received a new frame and chassis design along with a new center-port cylinder head and carburetor. The high-mounted exhaust system was still a single pipe, fed from the Siamese exhaust ports from the four-valve head, but it now graced the right side of the machine in a tight-fitting canister shape.

In 1978 the newly revised XL250S '78 replaced the original flagship, and in the following year the XL/XR500s replaced the original XL350s, as noted below.

Hot on the XL250s heels, the XL350K0 arrived in 1974, packing a five-speed, 348cc motor of 79 x 71-millimeter dimensions; compression was reduced to 8.3:1, and it was rated at 30 horsepower at 7,000 rpm. More than just a bore and stroke job of the XL250, the XL350 picked up an additional 41 pounds, weighing in at 321. The lighting systems were of a quick-disconnect design, allowing the bike to shed its street gear and go off-roading. Ignition was by a flywheel magneto, so a battery wasn't required for operation in the stripped-down mode. The 350s came out with the center-port intake-designed cylinder head and featured a low-slung single pipe and muffler system, mounted on the left side of the bike.

A larger 3.00x21 tire was fitted to the front end and there was a general strengthening of the whole machine, based on the lessons of the XL250s that came before. As with the XL250, the XL350 '76 models also received a revised chassis/frame, which carried through until the last of this species in 1978. In 1979 the XL350s were dropped in favor of all-new XL/XR500s with 33 horsepower, counterbalanced crankshafts, dual-exhaust port heads, 23-inch front wheels, and a weight-reduction to 260 and 282 pounds, respectively, for the new-generation 250s and 500s. The XL350 name came back in 1984 in the guise of a midrange machine, placed between the 250 and 500s.

Later (1984-on) models received six-speed transmissions, four-valve RFVC (radial valve arrangement) cylinder heads with split intake and exhaust ports. The intakes were fed by a progressive two-barrel carburetor system, and the exhaust had separate pipes for each port. The chassis was completely redesigned with the Pro-Link single-shock rear suspension systems and hydraulic disc brakes offered in 1984. Magneto ignition gave way to a new CDI system as well. These later machines represented a complete design break from the original models, and their basis can still be seen in today's models. Because the early XL250-350 machines were still not "serious" dirt bikes, many have survived in original condition and can often be found for less than $1,000. They can still be an inexpensive alternative to the current models, which cost $5,000 or more. These early bikes represent Honda's first real groundbreaking attempts to conquer the dirt and should be considered milestone bikes for those interested in Honda's off-road history.

The hefty SL350 twins were replaced by purposeful XL350 singles in 1974. These machines were a continuation of the first-generation XL250s, launched in 1972. The increased power of the 350 was offset by an increase in overall weight.

Honda made some interesting decisions at times, and the existence of the SL90 is an example. Taking the basic S90-CL90 powerplant, Honda designed a completely new chassis around it in the new 1969 Motosport fashion. The bike got a new larger carburetor and some other small engine improvements, but was basically the same as it was in other chassis. After all of this effort to make a new machine, Honda then replaced it with the completely new SL100 machines the following year. If you choose to restore an SL90, remember that not a lot of them are still around and the parts are even more scarce.

SL70-350 Motosports (1969–73)

Other than the early twin-cylinder SL350s (which retained the electric starter), the majority of SL-series Motosports machines were more seriously focused on the possibilities of occasional off-road adventures. New lightweight tube frames, long travel forks with dust seals rather than fork boots, 21-inch front wheels (in some cases), low-slung flat-black mufflers, and high-mounted fenders signaled their desire to leave the streets and head for the country. The good-looking SL70s headed the pack, followed by SL100/125 singles, 175 twins, and the 350 twin models.

XL/XR 70-650 (1972-on)

While the SL-series machines were a step in the right direction, the next generation of XL(street version) and XR(off-road version)-series of truly competitive on/off road machines (beginning in 1972 with the first XL250) showed Honda's commitment to serious, high-performance dirt-oriented motorcycles. This lineage extended to a whole family of XL/XR 70-650cc single-cylinder machines, many of which have continued into the new millennium. The 1979 XL-500 was the first really ground-breaking machine for the dirt, as Honda finally grew past the 350cc-sized thinking and went for the full half-liter–sized powerplant, but it was still housed in a dual-shock rear suspension chassis. Finally in 1981, Honda brought out its series of Pro-link, single shock rear suspension machines, showing its hand first on the XR200 bikes and then going across the board with 250-350-500cc versions in 1982.

With its five-speed transmission, big wheels, and good ground clearance, the SL100 Motosport offered a good balance of street and off-road riding. *Bill Orazio*

If you were raised on a Z50, then the next stop on your riding resume would be the XR-75 dirt bike. Finally, you got a clutch and four gears to play with in your quest for speed and excitement. The XR75 was one tough little machine. It's becoming increasingly hard to find examples of Honda's striking XR75 mini-MXer that haven't been crashed and abused by aspiring dirt racers.

TL125-250 (1973–76)

Honda supported what seemed to be an increased interest in Trials riding in the United States with its Trials bikes, offered for only four years (125—1973–73; 250—175–75). Honda had success in Europe with the Sammy Miller–inspired four-stroke factory competition machines and presented the TL125-250—a pair of production-based bikes for the Trials market. Although their appearance resembles the SL125/XL250 machines sold in the U.S., they didn't have a lot of common parts other than basic design.

The 1973 edition of the 122-cc Trials machine came without a lighting kit, which was only included in the last 1976 edition as a factory-installed system. *Bill Orazio*

The 1973 TL125 (and following K1 and K2 versions) series was loosely based on the street-legal SL125, but it had major modifications to the powerplant, which peaked at 8 horsepower at 8,000 rpm, down from the 12 horsepower at 9,000 rpm on the SL. TL125 peak torque was attained at only 4,000 rpm versus 8,000 rpm on the SL. Specially selected cylinder head, cam, and carburetion were responsible for reshaping the torque curve, as well as a lowered compression to 8:1 from the SL's 9.5:1. The TL125S '76 models received the revised two-piece cylinder head and a couple of extra ccs over the previous versions. A heavier flywheel was added to these machines to keep the momentum going while climbing terrain at walking speeds. The five-speed transmissions had special low-geared ratios for Trials-type riding.

The bodywork was slender and light, with all of the chassis components and gearing selected for slow-speed work. They were fitted with a

2.75x21 front tire and a 4.00x18 rear for maximum traction and agility. The TL125s were about 36 pounds lighter than the later XL125 street bike but a couple of pounds heavier than the base SL125 model.

The 1975–76 TL250 was based on the original XL250, introduced in 1972. Again, considerable modifications brought the power and torque peaks down out of the stratosphere. TL250 power and torque were 16.5 horsepower at 7,000 rpm and torque was at 5,500 rpm versus the XL's 22 horsepower at 8,000 rpm and torque peak at 8,000. The TL250 wheelbase was shortened by 3 inches, and the weight was brought down by almost 60 pounds to 218.

Both Kawasaki and Yamaha introduced some Trials machines to the United States, but neither were great sales successes. Other European-built machines were more purposeful-built and ultimately overshadowed Honda's four-strokers; however, the TL125 and 250s were fine reliable mounts for many enthusiasts just entering the sport and continue to be collected and restored today. It wasn't until the late 1980s that Honda reintroduced a similar machine, the TLR200 Reflex, which was street-legal but lasted only from 1986 to 1987, as a stablemate to the electric-starting TR200 Fatcat off-roader, featuring a 23.5 x 8.00 x 11-inch rear tire.

CR125/250 Elsinores (1973–75)

In 1973, Honda shocked the motocross community with the stunning CR250. At 214 pounds, the original silver-tanked Elsinore (named after the famed Elsinore GP) was also the most complete motocross/off-road bike on the market at the time. The next year a scaled-down CR125 was introduced with enormous success. The 125 was more evolved, featuring a six-speed transmission and leading axle forks.

Honda Elsinores came to the market during an era when you would typically buy a motocross bike and rebuild it to competitive specs before the bike ever saw a track. In stark contrast, the modern-looking Elsinores came with chrome-moly frames; lightweight, shoulderless, aluminum rims; race-ready suspension components;

Generous use of aluminum and race-ready suspension on Honda's CR-250 Elsinore ensured a season of successes right from the beginning. *AMA*

and CDI ignition. In addition, they didn't require removal of an oil injection system. Even the stock tires, grips, and control cables were top quality. All one had to do was put some numbers on the plates and race it. It was competitively priced, as well. Many a racing career was launched aboard a Honda Elsinore in the mid-seventies.

The Elsinore series of motocross bikes marked the first two-stroke, mass-production, off-road competition bike from Honda. It was also one of the most successful. In 1973 the CR250 was released as a two-year model. It possessed a highly tuned, piston-port, two-stroke engine that pumped out an impressive 33 horsepower at 7,500 rpm. The CR125 followed in 1974, with a six-speed transmission and leading axle forks. Both machines were equipped with more motocross innovations than any other bike at that time. A high-performance two-stroke engine, chrome-moly frame, race-ready suspension, and the very latest in motocross design theory were employed on these models. They also featured plastic fenders, form-fitting side panel number plates, and a great-looking polished aluminum fuel tank. These items needed to be purchased separately on the majority of other motocross machinery of the time.

The four distinct redesigns of the model between 1973 and 1980 are discussed below. The original silver tank 125 and 250 are highly sought after for vintage racing, restoring, and occasional trail riding. They are very collectable. A decent selection of parts is still available at your local Honda dealer and vintage bike specialists, who can be found in the American Historical Racing Motorcycle Association (AHRMA). Models from the 1976–78 era aren't allowed in some vintage racing associations, so check with your local promoter before purchasing an Elsinore from this era if you plan on entering vintage races.

Due to the quality design, great materials, and great performance, Honda Elsinores are desirable vintage and evolution class racers. The AHRMA regularly sanctions both vintage and evolution class racing throughout the United States. Elsinores and aftermarket parts are still readily available. For more information, schedules, memberships, and classifieds contact AHRMA, P.O. Box 676, Shawnee Mission, KS 66201.

The 1978–80 Elsinores are great selections for a new class called Evolution racing, with one caveat: these bikes featured a chrome bore cylinder that can't be bored to accept an oversize piston. The chrome bore cylinder is a good design, but everything has a life expectancy, including chrome bore cylinders. Inspect any potential cylinder on bikes from this era before you buy. If you find the cylinder is worn beyond specifications, you can contact one of the aftermarket piston and sleeve companies and see if they have replacement steel sleeve and oversized piston kits. One such company is Wiseco Piston, 7201 Industrial Park Blvd., Mentor, OH 44060, (440) 951-6600.

Four generations of Honda Elsinores were produced between 1973 and 1980. The following sections explain the differences and how to make a positive identification for proper year.

1973–1974 Elsinores

CR125: The 1974 and 1975 models are virtually the same bike. The fuel tank on the 1974 is green, while the 1975 units are identified by a splash of Honda racing red on top of the fuel tank and the number plates are red with black background for maximum racing number visibility.

In 1974, Honda jumped into the 125-cc motocross class in a big way with the CR125 Elsinore, a new, six-speed, two-stroke bike featuring beautiful alloy tank, chrome-moly frame, CDI ignition, and a host of race-only features. *Bill Orazio*

CR250: Released on February 1, 1973, this polished-aluminum-tanked beauty can be identified by the green stripes and silver number plates with green backgrounds. The exhaust is a down-swept unit with a small, pickle-shaped silencer.

1975–1978 Elsinores

CR125: A new heavy-duty swingarm dealt with the increased stress load of the forward-mounted rear shocks. A thicker, better-padded seat and improved polypropylene fender were also put to use. The 1977 models carried on the color theme with red fork boots and, in 1978, they featured red fork leg covers and rear shock springs.

CR250: There was a suspension revolution going on for dirt bikes at the time, and the new Honda featured a mild rear suspension treatment for increased suspension travel referred to at the time as "forward mount" shocks. As the bikes reached the end of their production run, they became increasingly red in color. The 1976 CR starts the trend with a red frame, tank, and side panels.

1979 Elsinores

CR125: The 125 was changed drastically, using the very latest in motocross technology at the time. Up front, a large 23-inch front wheel (typical motocross front wheels are 21 inch) was wrapped with Honda's exclusive claw action tires, which offered a unique tread design. The tires were poor, and the odd 23-inch front wheel lasted only one year. A good-looking bike, the 1979 featured a beautiful teardrop tank, molded side

panels, great fenders, heavy-duty swingarm, canted rear shocks (known as "layed down" shocks), and an all-new 124cc, reed-valve engine painted fire engine red. As futuristic as these bikes seemed to be, most folks didn't like the 23-inch front wheel and there was a lack of tire selection as well. This bike would be a great find for Evolution class racing.

CR250: In 1979, Honda once again shook the motocross community with its stunning new CR250R. Resembling the factory bikes at the time, they also featured "layed down" rear shocks. This shock angle eventually set the mold for any rear suspension design of this type. This line of bikes featured every innovation of the day all wrapped into one bike. They also featured one of the last beautiful aluminum fuel tanks in motocross. These bikes are also a good choice for Evolution class racing, although finding tires for 23-inch wheels is difficult.

1980 Elsinores

CR125: The fiercely competitive 125 class demanded that the 125 be redesigned for 1980. The 1979 model's 23-inch front wheel was replaced with a traditional 21-inch unit. The beautiful but fragile aluminum fuel tank was gone, replaced with a modern plastic tank. The rear suspension was upgraded with a set of gas-charged, remote reservoir shocks, mounted in an unusual position on a beefy swingarm. The last air-cooled CR125 engine proved to be one of the best 125 engines of the era, with an explosive midrange and plenty of over-rev.

Honda chose the "Elsinore" name for its two-stroke dirt bikes to commemorate the famous California race. While the name was used for both dual-purpose and motocross machines, it is the 250-cc motocross CR-250 Elsinore that people remember most today. *Bill Orazio*

CR250: An updated frame based on a works design graces the 1980 edition, as does a new center port exhaust. This is also the first Elsinore to feature a plastic fuel tank and FIM-spec number plates. Performance and parts-wise, this is an outstanding Evolution-class racer.

MT/MR125-175-250 Elsinores (1974–76)

Honda's successes with the CR125 and CR250 Elsinores led it to expand the line, in order to compete with other manufacturers' enduros, notably the Yamaha 125/175/250/360 Enduros.

In 1974 the street-legal, oil-injected, dual-shock MT125s and MT250s were launched, both continuing through 1976. These bikes were fully equipped with batteries, turn signals, horns, silenced intake and exhaust systems, and DOT-approved trials-type tires. About the same time, Honda added the MRs, a line of enduro and woods bikes, with tamed-down motors, adding speedometers and basic lighting packages. In 1977–78 a line of limited production 125cc roadracers were imported, based on the air-cooled CR125M Elsinore motocross racers.

MT125/250 Elsinores (1974–76)

MT125s were down to 13 horsepower from the original 21.7 of the racer and weighed in at 32 pounds heavier with the street gear and lighting equipment. The MT125s were equipped with only a

With its twin-shock rear suspension, six-speed transmission, and reed-valve motor, the 1980 CR80 was the first of the Pee-Wee-sized two-stroke motocrossers. Later models adopted PRO-LINK rear suspension and liquid-cooling. *AMA*

1.7-gallon fuel tank versus the 2.9 for the similar MR175. Obviously, this sets a short limit on the range for a street bike, even a relatively thrifty 125. Apparently, holding the theme relationship of the racers was of higher priority than the practicality of something with a little more capacity and range.

MT250s were down 10 horsepower from the CR250 version and gained an extra 47 pounds. The transmission was set up as a compromise between the CR and MR ratios for street use. Fuel capacity for the MT was only 2.2 gallons, so again there was a genuine limitation to the bikes' usable range. You weren't apt to see these machines on the highway, anyway, and many got stripped of their lights and were pressed into service as low-buck dirt machines.

MR175-250 Elsinores (1975–77)

MR175s were introduced in 1975, running three years, through the MR175 '77, while the MR250 1976 was a single year model. The MR-series Elsinore models were based on the CR125/250 Elsinore race bikes, but they were equipped with speedometers, larger fuel tanks, quieter USDA-approved spark arrestor exhausts, and were tuned for woods riding and enduro events. Equipped with magneto-powered lights (with stone

The MT125 Elsinore was a street-legal version of the CR125M Elsinore motorcrosser. A five-speed transmission and oil injection made for a usable look-alike ride of the famous motorcross racer. *AMA*

MR175s were based on the CR125 engines, but bored out to 175, then detuned (different porting, exhaust, and carb) for enduros and scrambles events. They featured bigger fuel tanks, magneto-powered lighting, speedometers with reset trip meters, and approved spark arrestor muffling systems. *AMA*

guards fitted to the headlights), they were not intended for street use. MR175s were 10-millimeter overbored 125s (actually 171cc), while the MR250s took their parentage from the CR250s. MR250s were given a 3.4-gallon fuel capacity, wide-ratio five-speed transmission, and they weighed 12 pounds less than their street-bike counterparts. MR250s were fed by a 34-millimeter power-jet carburetor, metering premixed fuel. MR175s and MT125s shared five-speed transmissions (but with different gear spreads), rather than the close-ratio six-speed from the CR125. Both machines were fitted with leading-axle forks. At the rear, MR175/250s wore finned, aluminum-bodied rear shocks.

Quite a few parts interchange between the basic models, and often there are cross-matched components in machines built for custom applications. Baja-racers need wide-ratio transmissions, excellent lights, and plenty of power, so all three objectives could be met with a

The MT250 was a street-legal version of the CR250 Elsinore racer, complete with oil injection and full street-legal lighting. *Bill Orazio*

proper selection of the right components from one of the three machines. Finding completely original examples of most dirt-oriented machines today is difficult, and few are being restored. A stock MR250, offered only in 1976 would be quite a find and worth having, if your interest leans toward the great outdoors. As useful riding bikes, they are limited in their appeal and of course have a short leash in regard to fuel capacity. The MRs did fulfill a function, as they drew more customers into the realm of off-road riding at several different levels of performance.

MR50 (1974–75)

Honda covered all the bases with the Elsinore lineup by creating a little miniature version called the MR50: a detuned, 50cc, three-speed, manual-clutch machine. It was probably dubbed MR for its low-speed capabilities, despite its CR high-speed, motocross looks. Certainly it was more capable of sustaining hours of dirt pounding than the four-stroke Z50 beginner models, with its larger wheel sizes and longer travel forks and rear shocks, which actually contained fluids. This bike was a logical step up from the companion model, the two-speed, auto-clutch, four-stroke QA-50, which had held the kid's bike torch aloft since 1970.

The 1975 MR50 Elsinore was the littlest Elsinore of them all, featuring three speeds and 50 cc of two-stroke fun made for the smallest of the Honda fans. The MR50 was produced for just two years. *AMA*

Collectible Roadracers

As Honda becamemore involved with roadracing at all levels, it chose to use the CR125M Elsinore motor as a basis for a Racing Service Center production-based 125cc-class roadracer. Despite the basic CR125M powerplant usage, many parts were unique to the needs of roadracing, including a close-ratio six-speed transmission (driving 415T x110-link chain), clip-on handlebars, expansion chamber, tachometer, and light-weight bodywork.

MT125R1 and R2 Roadracers (1977–78)

The R1 machine made 26 horsepower and used the rear wheel assembly (other than the alloy rim), forks, and cable-operated front disc-brake assembly from a CB125S1 street bike. All bodywork was fiberglass, including the tank, seat, fairing, and front fender. The overall dry weight was 154 pounds. The R2 had a revised expansion chamber, cylinder porting, cylinder head, and other modifications that boosted power to 28

Using CR125M Elsinore powerplants, MT125R road racers were capable of 105–110 miles per hour. The 1977 machines featured cable-operated front disc brakes, taken from the CB125S1 street machines. *AMA*

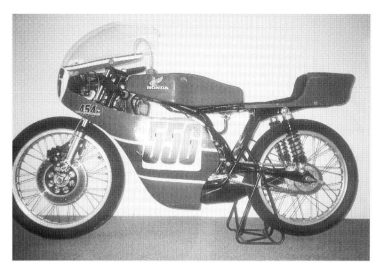

MT125R roadracers were imported for two years, from 1977 to 1978.

horsepower, as well as a slightly different seat and tank. The front disc brake was converted to hydraulic components with the caliper trailing the fork legs. Both Keihin and Mikuni carburetors were used on the first bikes; the Keihin getting the nod for the R2. The R2 models began with serial number 125R2E/F-1081, the 81st one built. RSC offered an optional R3 kit with a water-cooled top end, which added more power and kept it there throughout the race. Wheels were wire-spoke 18-inch hoops with narrow 2.50x18 tires for minimum rolling resistance.

Honda Racing Corporation (HRC) went head to head with Rotax-powered machines in the 600-cc flat track class with this RS600D, which uses a version of the four-valve-per-cylinder engine from the XL600s. *AMA*

135

This rare NS750 flat tracker, a factory-backed 750-cc V-twin, did battle with the reigning H-D racers in the early 1980s. Honda's first attempts in flat track racing were based on a heavily modified CX500 motor turned sideways! *AMA*

The MT125Rs faced the TZ125 Yamahas as their principal opponents in the 125cc racing classes, but Yamaha didn't support the class with great enthusiasm, so the Hondas ruled the roost for most of the late 1970s. Currently, Honda continues to supply 125cc racing with the RS125 bikes, which sit on fat 16-inch wheels and sport aluminum frames, disc brakes on both ends, and power plants offering 40+ horsepower. How times have changed!

CR750

Honda created a handful of factory-built CR750s to compete at the 1970 Daytona 200-mile roadrace event. This was meant to showcase their new model. Dick Mann won the race on the sole surviving machine and the event was a new milestone in Honda's racing history.

As a direct result of, and to support the 1970 race effort, Honda produced a limited number of CB750 "race kits," and made them available to their dealer network. The racing parts kit contained over 150 special parts, including everything from special cylinder head castings, slipper-skirt racing pistons, rings, valves, crankshaft, camshaft, pipes (4 separate megaphones), forks, brakes, gears, rims, spokes, sprockets, special gauges, carburetors, and a crank-driven magneto ignition. A hand-formed alloy fuel tank and oil tank, plus racing seat and fairing finished off the visual package.

The race parts in the kits were designated by a "970" suffix to the part number in Honda's parts locator system. The net result of installing

The four-valve, double overhead cam single in the CR110 production roadracer revs to 16,000 rpm and goes over 80 miles per hour , with an eight-speed transmission keeping it all on the narrow power peak! There was a street-legal version, as well, with a five-speed transmission and less peaky power curve.

the race kit was to raise the engine's output 23 horsepower to 90 horsepower, and the engine redline to 10,500 rpm, up 2,000 from stock.

Unfortunately, due to the limited number of kits manufactured, and a subsequent recall and destruction of many of these early parts by Honda of North America, assembling a kit CB750 Racing Type today is an extremely daunting task. A number of companies have specialized in making race parts for these bikes and they are still campaigned in AHRMA-sponsored races around the United States today.

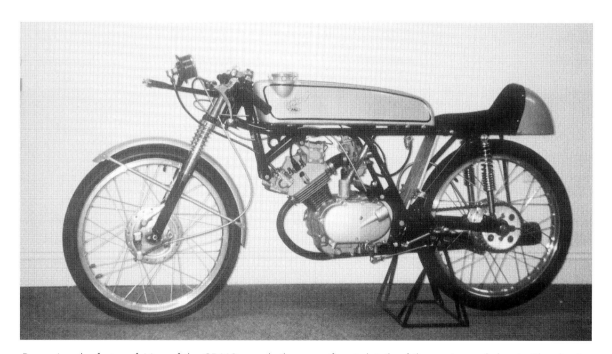

Removing the factory fairing of the CR110 reveals the magnificent details of the engine and chassis. The classic beauty of this machine actually inspired Honda to re-create it in a 1990s street machine, called the Dream 50, complete with double overhead cam four-valve cylinder head.

Some 220 125-cc, double overhead cam, five-speed CR93 production racers were produced, primarily in 1962. With engines that safely revved to 14,500 rpm, they were raced extensively in Japan and Europe for many years. Huge cylinder heads house gear-driven double overhead cams that operates four tiny valves per cylinder. The bore is 44 millimeters, and the engine stroke measures 41 millimeters. Restored bikes commonly fetch about $25,000 or more.

The rare street legal version of the CR93 production racer was created to fulfill the requirements of the Japanese racing associations that Honda's race bikes be based on street-legal machines. Probably fewer than 30 were produced.

In addition to production racers, street Hondas like this CB77 Super Hawk were often converted into race bikes.

Showing amazing flexibility for a huge manufacturer, Honda's racing department created three CR450s at the request of Bob Hansen, to compete within the AMA racing rules. Honda recast the cylinder heads in magnesium and added a suitable four-shoe front brake, in addition to many "one-off" modifications that allowed the bike to achieve 145-mile per hour track speeds. Two of the original three machines are known to exist. This one was restored and raced again 25 years later, taking a first place win at Daytona. *AMA*

When Honda decided to go road racing again, it tooled up some very special parts for the CB750. While there were a small batch of CR750s, an additional supply of replacement racing parts was made available to privateers to convert road machines into potent racers. Special bodywork, engines (including magnesium sand-cast carburetors and rear hub/brake), and chassis parts turned the CB750 street bike into a 90-horsepower rocketship. Cost of the kit parts in 1970 was $10,000, not including the motorcycle. *AMA*

Classic Racers (1959–67)

In 1962, Honda produced a small batch of CR (production road-racing) machines in 50, 125, 250, and 305cc displacements, including a tiny batch of street-legal 50cc and 125cc machines, with full lights and mufflers. The 125cc CR93 street bike still had the five-speed racing transmission and four-valve DOHC cylinder head, while the street version of the 50cc CR110 gave up its eight-speed gearbox for a five-speeder. The CR110 carried its four-valve DOHC cylinder head on the tiny engine that was shoehorned into the slender tube-frame chassis, riding on 2.00x18 tires.

Only a handful of CR72 (250cc) and CR77 (305cc) racers came to the United States. One CR72 bike was found in the Henry Ford museum and was chronicled in a story by Kevin Cameron, then an editor for *Cycle* magazine. Cameron produced one of his usual highly detailed articles covering the actual specifications of the machine and how it came to be that way, from the viewpoint of Honda engineering. Almost all of the CR72-77s are back in Japan, bought up by investors back in the 1980s. One lone example continues to be shown and raced in AHRMA vintage roadraces by Peter Johnson, who is fortunately a master machinist, which is necessary due to the unavailability of parts support for this rare bike. What a great treat it is to be able to see and hear this magnificent racing machine, almost 40 years after its birth. It is probably the last running example in North America now, and perhaps the last one in the United States.

One must not confuse these CR bikes with the RC-designated, factory-sponsored, race-team bikes, ridden by famous riders including Hailwood, Redman, Tavari, Bryans, and many others. The RC bikes were continually upgraded over the years and all classes had multicylindered entries, ranging from 50cc twins to the five-cylinder 125 and ultimately the 250-350cc sixes. Honda also fielded some 500cc fours late in the game, but those were of limited success. For the most part, none of the factory-backed machines is for sale, as most have been acquired for restoration and display at Honda's museum in Suzuka.

Honda's Race to the Top

In addition to participating in (and winning) some Japanese National races in the late 1950s, Soichiro Honda vowed at a March 1954 dealers' meeting to send a team of Honda roadracers to the Isle of Man (IOM) TT races. By 1959 the Honda racing team brought a number of 125cc roadracers to the Island course and gained a sixth place, plus the 125cc team prize, with four bikes finishing the race. It was a fair start for a new team and newly designed machinery. The

Victor World, CB750 expert, gets up to speed on his CR750 replica. Restored CB750 racers can often be seen at current AHRMA racing events.

Luigi Taveri earned a 125-cc World Championship on this RC 149, a 125-cc five-cylinder, 20,000-rpm, eight-speed, 34-horsepower factory racer.

original bevel-drive, DOHC RC 141 125cc race bikes had two-valve cylinder heads and proved to be unsatisfactory, so new four-valve heads were flown in to raise the power output to 18.5 horsepower at 14,000 rpm. A six-speed transmission was used to keep the engine up on the top of the narrow powerband.

The front suspension was still a leading-link style and was unsuitable for racing, particularly at the Island road course. When Honda came back in 1960 with the 20 horsepower RC 143, the bike had telescopic front forks, which greatly improved the handling characteristics. Even with all the improvements, the 1960 effort only yielded another sixth place for rider Naomi Tanaguchi, who had raced there the year before.

The 1960 race also saw the debut of the new 250cc RC161 four-cylinder machine, which was making about 40 horsepower at 13,000 rpm. The bike failed to finish the race at the IOM but finally achieved a third-place finish at the German GP race in July. Honda had a double win in September of that year in England. Both the 125 and 250 won their classes at that event, causing great pride for the Honda race team.

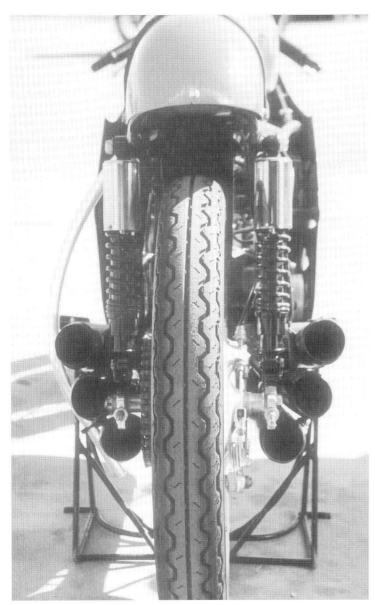

It is only safe to take this photo of this bike when the engine is not running! This rear view of a world championship winner shows the business end of a famous historic racing machine, capable of some 18,000 rpm and about a million decibel noise output. If you ever heard one running, you will never forget the sound.

The GP Season

In 1961 it was an all-Honda show, with the teams taking both the 125 and 250 championships and signing ace racer, Mike Hailwood, to the team. The combination of man and machine was too great for the opposition and foreshadowed Honda's domination in world roadracing for years to come.

In 1962 the FIM added a 50cc class and Honda stepped in with a modified version of its CR110 single, labeled the RC111, which made 9.5 horsepower at 14,400 rpm. However, Suzuki and Kreidler fielded fast two-strokes and Honda failed to win the championship in that class. At the end of the year, however, Honda unveiled a new 50cc twin machine, still with DOHC four-valve heads, and the new RC112 made 10 horsepower at an astonishing 17, 000 rpm and fed a nine-speed transmission. By the 1966 season, the final version machine, a RC 114, made 12 horsepower at 19,000 rpm and went 105 miles per hour, all from a scant 3-ci engine displacement.

The 125cc RC bikes remained as twins until 1963, when the new four-cylinder bikes were brought out to counter the increasingly intense competition, especially from the dominant Suzuki of Hugh Anderson, and later in 1966 by the Yamahas of Bill Ivy and Phil Read. By 1966, the final model RC149 five-cylinder machine made 34 horsepower at 20,500 rpm and could achieve more than 126 miles per hour. Honda's relentless pursuit of engineering excellence brought the weight of the five-cylinder bike down to 18 pounds below the weight of the first RC143 twin!

The 250cc class bikes, beginning with the early RC161 four, eventually developed into the howling 60 horsepower at 18,000 rpm six, with a seven-speed gearbox. Winners of dozens of races and numerous world championships at the hands of Jim Redman and Mike Hailwood, the mighty six was almost invincible in the 1966 world championships. The engine concept was stretched to fill the 350cc classes only at the 1967 season, as the earlier four-cylinder powerplant had been sufficient to ward off the competition until 1966. The 350 six was only a 297cc version of the 250, giving up some 5 horsepower to the previous full-sized four, but the design gave an extra 3,000 rpm of powerband to work with and was an ultimate success with Mike Hailwood in the saddle.

Honda came up short with a newly designed 500cc class four-cylinder machine in 1966–67, though. Despite making over 85 horsepower at 12,500 rpm, the chassis was never able to cope with this much thrust, and despite Hailwood's heroic efforts to keep it on track, the bike was defeated due to a combination of ill-handling and mechanical misfortune. Hailwood even commissioned a new frame to be built in England for the machine, but Honda wouldn't consider using it, so the effort was for naught. Despite Hailwood's brilliant talent, he finished second in both the 1966 and 1967 500cc championship seasons.

Honda came back each year with more ideas and more cylinders that made more power. By 1966, Honda took all the Championship titles in the 50cc, 125cc, 250cc, 350cc, and 500cc classes, an unprecedented event in racing history. One could suppose that if the FIM had not finally restricted the number of cylinders per class, we might have seen a ten-cylinder, 250cc racer, made from a doubled-up 125cc five! By the way, the smaller displacement machines were all capable of sustaining over 20,000 rpm during a race. During testing of one of the 24cc power units (before it was coupled with four more of the same to give 125cc), it was discovered that only 85 octane fuel was sufficient to operate an engine at 20,000 rpm. This is the stuff of the imaginative mind of Soichiro Honda and company, and just an example of why so many enthusiasts are fans of the Honda motorcycles.

Honda wins all five

50cc · 125cc · 250cc

350cc · 500cc

World Grand Prix Championships

For the first time in motorcycle racing history — a single manufacturer has won all five International Grand Prix championships: the 50, 125, 250, 350 and 500cc classes! Even in the rugged 500cc class, Honda ended the year with more championship points over all nine races than any other make — and this in its first year of competition in this class!

But a great finish to the Grand Prix year such as this for Honda is really a beginning for you. For it's from this point on that Honda is able to take the new ideas in motorcycle design it has learned over a year of grueling competition and apply them to refinements in street machines such as yours. Or the ones you can buy from any of Honda's more than 1700 dealers from coast to coast.

See your Honda dealer now — and find out what makes Honda, year in and year out, the world's greatest motorcycle buy.

HONDA

world's biggest seller!

The combination of winning machinery and top-level riding paid off for Honda when it earned a place in racing history by winning all five World Grand Prix Championship classes in 1966.

Performance Specifications for Honda Factory Roadracing Motorcycles

50cc Class Roadracers

Model	RC111
Year	1964
Horsepower	9.5 @ 14K rpm
Redline	16K rpm
Cylinders	1
Valves	2
Bore x stroke	40 x 39mm
Displacement	49cc
Compression	10.5:1
Gearbox	6-speed
Weight	125 lb
Top speed	78 mph

Model	RC112
Year	Late 1964
Horsepower	10 @ 17.5K rpm
Redline	18.5K rpm
Cylinders	2
Valves	4
Bore x stroke	33 x 29mm
Displacement	49.6cc
Compression	10.5:1
Gearbox	9-speed
Weight	137 lb
Top speed	84 mph

Model	RC113
Year	1963
Horsepower	10 @ 17.5K rpm
Redline	18.5K rpm
Cylinders	2
Valves	4
Bore x stroke	33 x 29mm
Displacement	49.6cc
Compression	11:1
Gearbox	9-speed
Weight	110 lb
Top speed	84 mph

Model	RC114
Year	1964
Horsepower	12 @ 19K rpm
Redline	20K rpm
Cylinders	2
Valves	4
Bore x stroke	33 x 29mm
Displacement	49.6cc
Compression	11.5:1
Gearbox	9-speed
Weight	110 lb
Top speed	90 mph

Model	RC114
Year	Late 1964
Horsepower	12 @ 19K rpm
Redline	20K rpm
Cylinders	2
Valves	4
Bore x stroke	33 x 29mm
Displacement	49.6cc
Compression	12:1
Gearbox	9-speed
Weight	110 lb
Top speed	90 mph

Model	RC115
Year	1965
Horsepower	13 @ 20K rpm
Redline	21K rpm
Cylinders	2
Valves	4
Bore x stroke	43 x 27.8 mm
Displacement	49.8cc
Compression	12:1
Gearbox	9-speed
Weight	110 lb
Top speed	90 mph

Model	RC116
Year	1966
Horsepower	14 @ 21.5K rpm
Redline	22.5K rpm
Cylinders	2
Valves	4
Bore x stroke	35.5 x 25.14mm
Displacement	49.77cc
Compression	12:1
Gearbox	9-speed
Weight	110 lb
Top speed	105 mph

125cc Class Roadracers

Model	RC142
Year	1959
Horsepower	18 @ 13K rpm
Redline	14K rpm
Cylinders	2
Valves	4
Bore x stroke	44 x 41mm
Displacement	124.6 cc
Compression	10.5:1
Gearbox	6-speed
Weight	192 lb
Top speed	108+ mph

Model	RC143
Year	1960
Horsepower	18 @ 13K rpm
Redline	14K rpm
Cylinders	2
Valves	4
Bore x stroke	44 x 41mm
Displacement	124.6cc
Compression	10.5:1
Gearbox	6-speed
Weight	205 lb
Top speed	108+ mph

Model	RC143(2)
Year	Late 1961
Horsepower	23 @ 13K rpm
Redline	14K rpm
Cylinders	2
Valves	4
Bore x stroke	42 x 45mm
Displacement	124.6cc
Compression	10.5:1
Gearbox	6-speed
Weight	226 lb
Top speed	108+ mph

Model	RC144
Year	1961
Horsepower	23 @ 14K rpm
Redline	14K rpm
Cylinders	2
Valves	4
Bore x stroke	42 x 45mm
Displacement	124.6cc
Compression	10.5:1
Gearbox	6-speed
Weight	N/A
Top speed	108 mph

Model	RC145
Year	1962
Horsepower	24 @ 14K rpm
Redline	15K rpm
Cylinders	2
Valves	4
Bore x stroke	44 x 44mm
Displacement	124.6cc
Compression	10.5:1
Gearbox	6-speed
Weight	213 lb
Top speed	108+ mph

Model	RC146
Year	1963
Horsepower	27 @ 17K rpm
Redline	18K rpm
Cylinders	4
Valves	4
Bore x stroke	35 x 32mm
Displacement	123.15cc
Compression	10.5:1
Gearbox	7-speed
Weight	192 lb
Top speed	108+ mph

Model	RC146(2)
Year	1964
Horsepower	28 @ 18K rpm
Redline	19K rpm
Cylinders	4
Valves	4
Bore x stroke	35 x 32mm
Displacement	123.15cc
Compression	10.5:1
Gearbox	7-speed
Weight	192 lb
Top speed	108+ mph

Model	RC148
Year	1965
Horsepower	32 @ 20K rpm
Redline	21K rpm
Cylinders	5
Valves	4
Bore x stroke	34 x 27.5mm
Displacement	124.5cc
Compression	12:1
Gearbox	8-speed
Weight	187 lb
Top speed	120 mph

Model	RC149
Year	1966
Horsepower	34 @ 20K rpm
Redline	21K rpm
Cylinders	5
Valves	4
Bore x stroke	34 x 27mm
Displacement	124.5cc
Compression	12:1
Gearbox	8-speed
Weight	187 lb
Top speed	126 mph

250cc Class Roadracers

Model	RC161
Year	1960
Horsepower	35 @ 14K rpm
Redline	15K rpm
Cylinders	4
Valves	4
Bore x stroke	44 x 41mm
Displacement	249.37cc
Compression	10.5:1
Gearbox	6-speed
Weight	281 lb
Top speed	132+ mph

Model	RC162
Year	1961
Horsepower	45 @ 14K rpm
Redline	15K rpm
Cylinders	4
Valves	4
Bore x stroke	44 x 41mm
Displacement	249.37cc
Compression	10.5:1
Gearbox	6-speed
Weight	278 lb
Top speed	132+ mph

Model	RC163
Year	1962
Horsepower	46 @ 14K rpm
Redline	15K rpm
Cylinders	4
Valves	4
Bore x stroke	44 x 41mm
Displacement	249.37cc
Compression	10.5:1
Gearbox	6-speed
Weight	281 lb
Top speed	132+ mph

Model	RC164
Year	1963
Horsepower	Info N/A
Redline	15K rpm
Cylinders	4
Valves	4
Bore x stroke	44 x 41mm
Displacement	249.37cc
Compression	10.5:1
Gearbox	6-speed
Weight	275 lb
Top speed	132+ mph

Model	RC165
Year	1965
Horsepower	50 @ 14K rpm
Redline	19K rpm
Cylinders	6
Valves	4
Bore x stroke	39 x 34mm
Displacement	249.42cc
Compression	12.5:1
Gearbox	7-speed
Weight	242 lb
Top speed	145+ mph

Model	RC166
Year	1966
Horsepower	55 @ 18K rpm
Redline	19K rpm
Cylinders	4
Valves	4
Bore x stroke	39 x 34mm
Displacement	249.37cc
Compression	10.5:1
Gearbox	7-speed
Weight	246 lb
Top speed	132+ mph

Model	RC167
Year	1967
Horsepower	60 @ 18K rpm
Redline	19K rpm
Cylinders	4
Valves	4
Bore x stroke	41 x 31.5mm
Displacement	249.52cc
Compression	10.5:1
Gearbox	7-speed
Weight	250 lb
Top speed	132+ mph

350cc Class Roadracers

Model	RC170
Year	1962
Horsepower	49 @ 14K rpm
Redline	15K rpm
Cylinders	4
Valves	4
Bore x stroke	47 x 41mm
Displacement	284cc
Compression	10.5:1
Gearbox	6-speed
Weight	288 lb
Top speed	153+ mph

Model	RC171
Year	1963
Horsepower	50 @ 12K rpm
Redline	14K rpm
Cylinders	4

Valves	4
Bore x stroke	49 x 45mm
Displacement	339cc
Compression	10.5:1
Gearbox	6-speed
Weight	288 lb
Top speed	144+ mph

Model	RC172
Year	1963/64
Horsepower	53 @ 13K rpm
Redline	14K rpm
Cylinders	4
Valves	4
Bore x stroke	50 x 44.5mm
Displacement	349.5cc
Compression	10.5:1
Gearbox	6-speed
Weight	290 lb
Top speed	138+ mph

Model	RC172(2)
Year	1965
Horsepower	60 @ 13K rpm
Redline	14K rpm
Cylinders	4
Valves	4
Bore x stroke	50 x 44.5mm
Displacement	349.5cc
Compression	10.5:1
Gearbox	6-speed
Weight	297 lb
Top speed	138+ mph

Model	RC173
Year	1966
Horsepower	70 @ 14K rpm
Redline	15K rpm
Cylinders	4
Valves	4
Bore x stroke	50 x 44.5mm
Displacement	284cc
Compression	10.5:1
Gearbox	6-speed
Weight	317 lb
Top speed	150+ mph

Model	RC174
Year	1967
Horsepower	65 @ 17K rpm
Redline	18K rpm
Cylinders	6
Valves	4
Bore x stroke	41 x 37.5mm
Displacement	297cc
Compression	10.5:1
Gearbox	7-speed
Weight	259 lb
Top speed	150+ mph

500cc Class Roadracers

Model	RC181
Year	1966
Horsepower	85 @ 12K rpm
Redline	12.5K rpm
Cylinders	4
Valves	4
Bore x stroke	57 x 48mm
Displacement	489.94cc
Compression	11.5:1
Gearbox	6-speed
Weight	336 lb
Top speed	156+ mph

Model	RC181
Year	1967
Horsepower	85 @ 12K rpm
Redline	13K rpm
Cylinders	4
Valves	4
Bore x stroke	57.56 x 48mm
Displacement	499cc
Compression	11.5:1
Gearbox	6-speed
Weight	332 lb
Top speed	153+ mph

Specifications

Specifications
Models: CB/CL160

CB 1964–69
CL 1966–67

Engine	4-stroke, OHC, parallel-twin, twin-carburetors
Bore x stroke	50x41 mm (1.97x1.61 ci)
Displacement	161cc (9.84 ci)
Lubrication	Wet-sump, plunger pump
Compression ratio	8.5:1
Horsepower	16.5 @ 10,000 rpm
Transmission	4-speed, constant-mesh
Shift	Left foot
Shift pattern	Down for low, 3 up from neutral
Primary drive	Gear-driven
Clutch	Multi-plate, wet
Gear ratios:	
4th	1.040:1
3rd	1.318:1
2nd	1.778:1
1st	2.769:1
Wheelbase	1,277 mm (50.3 in.)
Suspension:	
Front	Telescopic fork
Rear	Swingarm, dual shocks
Weight	127 kg (280 lb.)
Fuel capacity	10.4 liters (2.7 gal)
Oil capacity	1 liter (1.25 qt.)
Top speed	70+ mph

Models: CB/CL160

Collectibility	★★★
Cruising speed	50 mph
Comfort of ride	★★★
Passenger accommodations	★★
Reliability	★★★★
Parts/Service availability	★★

Text Comments:

"Baby Super Hawks" were what CB160s were often called. Styling was undeniably shaped after their bigger brothers. They were a little overweight, but their pinpoint handling and powerful DLS front brakes kept them out in front of the competition.

Specifications
Models: CB350/400 Four

350 1972-74
400 1975-77

Engine	4-stroke, SOHC, inline, four-cylinder
Bore x stroke:	(350) 47x50 mm (1.85x1.969 ci)
	(400) 51x50 mm (2.008x1.969 ci)
Displacement:	(350) 347cc
	(400) 408cc
Lubrication	Wet-sump, pressure fed
Compression ratio:	(350) 9.3:1
	(400) 9.4:1
Horsepower:	(350) 32
	(400) 37
Transmission:	(350) 5-speed, constant-mesh
	(400) 6-speed, constant-mesh
Shift	Left foot
Shift pattern	Down for low;
	(350) Four up from neutral
	(400) Five up from neutral
Primary drive	Chain
Clutch	Multi-plate, wet
Gear ratios:	(350)
5th	.965:1
4th	1.148:1
3rd	1.416:1
2nd	1.850:1
1st	2.773:1
	(400)
6th	.866:1
5th	.965:1
4th	1.111:1
3rd	1.375:1
2nd	1.800:1
1st	2.733:1
Wheelbase	1,355 mm (53.5 in.)
Suspension:	
Front	Telescopic
Rear	Swingarm, dual shocks
Weight	375 lb.
Fuel capacity:	(350) 12 liters (3.2 gal)
	(400) 14 liters (3.7 gal)
Oil capacity	3.7 qt.
Top speed	95-105 mph

Models: CB350F/CB400F

Collectibility	(350) ★★★★
	(400) ★★★★★
Cruising speed	70 mph
Comfort of ride	★★★
Passenger accommodations	★★★
Reliability	★★★★★
Parts/Service availability	★★

Text Comments:

Smallest of Honda's fours, the 350 was released in 1973. Smooth, quiet, and nimble, it suffered from an unfavorable power-to-weight ratio.

The CB400F was a quantum leap ahead of the 350, and had more everything . . . displacement, horsepower, six-speed transmission , 4-Into-1 exhaust and classic cafe' style!

Specifications

Models: CB/CL350

1968–73

Engine	4-stroke, SOHC, parallel-twin, twin-carburetors
Bore x stroke	64x50.6 mm (2.52x1.922 ci)
Displacement	325cc (19.8 ci)
Lubrication	Plunger-type
Compression ratio	9.5:1
Horsepower:	(CB) 36 @ 10,500 rpm
	(CL) 33 @ 9,500 rpm
Transmission	5-speed, constant-mesh
Shift	Left foot
Shift pattern	Down for low, 4 up from neutral
Primary drive	Gear-driven
Clutch	Multi-plate, wet
Gear ratios:	5th .900:1
	4th 1.036:1
	3rd 1.269:1
	2nd 1.636:1
	1st 2.353:1
Wheelbase	52.0 in.
Suspension:	Front Telescopic fork
	Rear Swingarm, dual shock
Weight:	(CB) 345 lb.
	(CL) 352 lb.
Fuel capacity	(CB) 12 liters (3.2 gal)
	(CL) 9 liters (2.4 gal)
Oil capacity	2.0 qt.
Top speed:	(CB) 100 mph
	(CL) 90 mph

Model: CB/CL350

Collectibility	★★★
Cruising speed	65 mph
Comfort of ride	★★★
Passenger accommodations	★★★
Reliability	★★★
Parts/Service availability	★★

Text Comments:

In 1968 the 350s replaced the long-running 305s, in both CB and CL form. New transmissions featured a 5th ratio and the chain-driven primary was replaced with a gear-drive. A plunger-type oil pump was driven off the back of the clutch basket. Rubber-diaphragm, constant-velocity (CV) carburetors made their debut on this model too.

Specifications

Models: CB/CJ/CL360

Years:

(CL) 1974–75

(CJ) 1974–76

Engine	4-stroke, SOHC, parallel-twin, dual 30-mm carburetors
Bore x stroke	67x50.6 mm (2.61x1.97 in.)
Displacement	356cc (22 ci)
Lubrication	Trichoid oil pump, centrifugal, screen filter
Compression ratio	9.3:1
Horsepower	34 @ 9,000 rpm
Transmission	(CB,CL) 6-speed, constant-mesh
	(CJ)5-speed, constant-mesh
Shift	Left foot
Shift pattern	Down for low, 4 up from neutral
Primary drive	Gear-driven
Clutch	Multi-plate, wet
Gear ratios:	6th .886:1
	5th .965:1
	4th 1.111:1
	3rd 1.375:1
	2nd 1.667:1
	1st 2.438:1
Wheelbase	52.6 in.
Wheels:	Front 3.00x18-in.
	Rear 3.50x18-in.
Suspension:	Front Telescopic fork
	Rear Swingarm, dual shocks
Weight:	(CB/CL) 364 lb.
	(CJ) 351 lb.
Fuel capacity:	(CB/CL) 2.9 gal
	(CJ) 3.7 gal
Oil capacity	2.1 qt.
Top speed	105 mph

Models: CB/CL360

Collectibility	★
Cruising speed	65 mph
Comfort of ride	★★★
Passenger accommodations	★★★
Reliability	★★★
Parts/Service availability	★★

Text Comments:

This model was a 1974 replacement for the popular CB/CL350. New features included a standard front disc brake on CB360T models (drum on CL and CJ versions) and a 6-speed transmission on CB/CL360. It offered steady, but unspectacular performance.

The CJ360 had a 5-speed transmission and deleted the center stand and electric starter. It also featured a new 2-Into-1 exhaust and restyled tank, fenders and seat. This model was available for 2-years.

Specifications

Models: CB500/550

1971–1978

Engine	4-stroke, SOHC, inline four-cylinder
Bore x stroke	56x50.6 mm (2.205x1.992 ci)
Displacement	498cc (30.38 ci)
Lubrication	Pressure-fed, trichoid oil pump
Compression ratio	9.0:1
Horsepower	50 @ 9,000 rpm
Transmission	5-speed, constant-mesh
Shift	Left side, foot
Shift pattern	Down for low, 4 up from neutral
Primary drive	Multi-plate chain, reduction 2:1
Clutch	Multi-plate, wet
Gear ratios:	5th .900:1
	4th 1.036:1
	3rd 1.269:1
	2nd 1.636:1
	1st 2.353:1
Wheelbase	55.3 in.
Wheels:	Front 3.25x19-in.
	Rear 3.50x18-in.
Suspension:	Front Telescopic fork
	Rear Swingarm, dual shock
Weight	407 lb.
Fuel capacity	14 liters (3.7 gal)
Oil capacity	3.2 qt.
Fuel consumption	average
Top speed	110 mph

Models: CB500/550

Collectibility	★★★★
Cruising speed	75 mph
Comfort of ride	★★★★
Passenger accommodations	★★★
Reliability	★★★★
Parts/Service availability	★★★

Text Comments:

Honda's next four-cylinder model release after the CB750. Engine assembly is 24 lb. lighter than the 750 motor. The bike weighed 403.5 lb., while the CB750 tipped the scales at 517 lb. Featuring a lower weight and seat height, this bike opened up the market for riders seeking smooth engine performance in a more compact chassis. Engine was bored to 550cc in 1974. Restyled cosmetics and a new exhaust system were mounted in 1977–78. These bikes were characterized as fun to ride, smooth, average power for size and very reliable.

Specifications

Models: C100 Super Cub/CA100

Honda 50

1958–69

Engine	4-stroke, OHV, horizontal single-cylinder
Bore x stroke	40x39 mm (1.57x1.53 ci)
Displacement	49cc (3.0 ci)
Lubrication	Wet-sump, splash fed
Compression ratio	8.5:1
Horsepower	4.5 @ 9,500 rpm
Transmission	3-speed
Shift	Left foot, heel/toe shifter
Shift pattern	Down for low, 2 down from neutral
Primary drive	Gear-driven
Clutch	Multi-plate, wet, automatic
Gear ratios:	3rd 12.8:1
	2nd 19.3:1
	1st 35.8:1
Wheelbase	1.180 mm (46.5 in.)
Wheels	2.25x17-in. front and rear
Suspension:	Front Leading-link
	Rear Swingarm, dual shock
Weight	143 lb.
Fuel capacity	3.0 liters (.08 gal)
Oil capacity	.6 liters (1.4 pt)
Fuel consumption	(225 mpg @ 18 mph average
Top speed: estimated	43.5 mph

Models: C/CA100

Collectibility	★★★★
Cruising speed	35 mph
Comfort of ride	★★
Passenger acco mmodations	★
Reliability	★★★
Parts/Service availability	★★

Text Comments:

This is the bike that started it all, especially in the United States. If your parents wouldn't let you buy a "motorcycle," they would probably let you buy a Honda 50! Priced as low as $245 each, Honda marketed them to teenagers and college kids. Imagine going 200 miles on a gallon of $.25 gasoline in those days! It was almost cheaper than walking! Honda has made over 25 million Cubs, in one version or the other, since 1958.

Specifications

Model: CB650

1979–82

Engine	4-stroke, SOHC inline, four-cylinder	
Bore x stroke	59.8x55.8 mm (2.39x2.23 ci)	
Displacement	627cc (37.6 ci)	
Lubrication	Pressure-fed, trichoid pump	
Compression ratio	9.0:1	
Horsepower	63 @ 9,000 rpm	
Transmission	5-speed, constant-mesh	
Shift	Left foot	
Shift pattern	Down for low, 4 up from neutral	
Primary drive	Chain	
Clutch	Multi-plate, wet	
Wheelbase	56.3-in.	
Wheels:	Front	3.25x19-in.
	Rear	3.75x18-in.
Suspension:	Front	Hydraulic fork
	Rear	Swingarm, dual shocks
Weight	436 lb.	
Fuel capacity	18 liters	
Oil capacity	3.5 qt.	
Fuel consumption	average	
Top speed	120 mph	

Model CB650

Collectibility	★★
Cruising speed	75 mph
Comfort of ride	★★★★
Passenger accommodations	★★★
Reliability	★★★
Parts/Service availability	★★

Text Comments:

Engine is based on the CB500-550, but bored and stroked to 627cc. New carburetors, exhaust, and internal engine redesigns resulted in a startling power increase over previous machines. Good value for the money, but they got lost in the lineup of new DOHC fours and shaft-drive twins.

Specifications

Models S90/CL90

1964–69

Engine	4-stroke, OHC, horizontal, single-cylinder	
Bore x stroke	50 (1.97)x45 mm (1.80)	
Displacement	89.6cc (5.47 ci)	
Lubrication	Wet-sump, pressure-fed, trichoidal-type, screen/centrifugal filter	
Compression ratio	8.2:1	
Horsepower	8 @ 9,500 rpm	
Transmission	4-speed, constant-mesh, return-type	
Shift	Left side, heel-toe shifter	
Shift pattern	Down for low, 3 up from neutral	
Primary drive	Gear-driven	
Clutch	Multi-plate, wet	
Gear ratios:	4th	.88:1
	3rd	1.09:1
	2nd	1.53:1
	1st	2.54:1
Wheelbase	1,195 mm (47.08-in.)	
Wheels	2.50x18-in., front and rear	
Suspension:	Front	Telescopic, hydraulic damped
	Rear	Swingarm, dual shocks
Dry weight	86.5 kg (190 lb. S90); 92 kg (202 lb. CL90)	
Fuel capacity	7.0 liter (1.75 US gal S90) 7.5 liter (2.0 US gal CL90)	
Oil capacity	.9 liter (1 qt.)	
Fuel consumption	75 km/liter @ 35 kmh 176 mpg @ 25 mph average	
Top speed	62 mph	

Models: S90/CL90

Collectibility	****
Cruising speed	50 mph
Comfort of ride	***
Passenger accommodation	**
Reliability	****
Parts/Service availability	**

Text Comments:

S90 and CL90 Hondas were the "backbone" of the lightweight models from the mid-60s to 1970. Their T-shaped "backbone" stamped-steel frames were light and rugged. In the 1960s, teenagers adored these machines. Many new riders worked their way up the ladder of larger-displacement Hondas on these bikes. The simple, rugged, OHC 90cc engines were made by the millions and the reliability was unsurpassed in the small-bike market.

Specifications

Model: CB92 Benly Super Sports

1960–64

Engine	4-stroke, parallel, 30-degree inclined vertical tw in.
Bore x stroke	44 x41 mm (1.73x1.61 ci) (1.73 in.) x 41 mm (1.61 in.)
Displacement	124cc (7.59 ci)
Lubrication	Wet-sump, pressure-fed, screen and centrifugal filter
Compression ratio	10:1
Horsepower	15 @ 10,500 rpm
Transmission	4-speed, constant-mesh
Shift	Left side, return change, heel-toe shifter
Shift pattern	Down for low, 3 up from neutral
Primary drive	Gear-driven
Clutch	Multi-plate, manual
Gear ratios:	4th	8.98:1
	3rd	11.12:1
	2nd	15.72:1
	1st	25.24:1
Wheelbase	1,260 mm (49.64-in.)
Wheels:	Front	2.50x18-in.
	Rear	2.75x18-in.
Suspension:	Front	Leading-link
	Rear	Swingarm, dual shocks
Weight	110 kg (220 lb.)
Fuel capacity	10.5 liters (2.8 gal)
Oil capacity	.8 liter (1 qt.)
Fuel consumption	65 km/ liter @ 35 kph, 185 mpg at 22 mph average
Top speed	130 kph (80 mph)

Model: CB92 Benly Super Sports

Collectibility	*****
Cruising speed	60 mph
Comfort of ride	**
Passenger accommodations	*
Reliability	**
Parts/Service availability	*

Text Comments:

Despite the Benly-type (leading-link) front suspension, the CB92s were rough riders on the street. Stiffly sprung, they buck and jump around on an average paved road. The sculpted arrowhead-shaped fuel tank allowed tucking in your knees at speed, but the hard and narrow seats didn't offer much long-distance comfort. Cold-blooded and high-strung (even in street form), the addition of YB racing parts caused them to be even more uncomfortable on public roads. They did possess great brakes, though, and the unique styling catches interested glances wherever they are seen. If you have a chance to hear one that is equipped with factory megaphones, you will be amazed by the sound coming from such a small bike.

They had a great racing history in the beginning of Honda's racing days in the United States and have become rare due to the combination of wearing them out, exporting them to Japan and the fact that only about 1,051 of them were sold in the United States from 1960–62. Production and sales continued until 1964.

Specifications

Models: CB72/77

1961–67

Engine	4-stroke, SOHC, parallel-twin
Carburetion:	(CB72) Dual, 22 mm
	(CB77) Dual, 26 mm
Bore x stroke:	(CB72) 54x54 mm
	(CB77) 60x54 mm
Displacement:	(CB72) 247cc, 15 ci
	(CB77) 305cc, 21 ci
Lubrication	Wet-sump, gear-driven, centrifugal/screen filter
Compression ratio	8.5:1
Horsepower:	(CB72) 24 @ 9,000 rpm
	(CB77) 28 @ 9,000 rpm
Transmission	4-speed, constant-mesh
Shift	left foot
Shift pattern	Down for low, 3 up from neutral
Primary drive	Chain
Clutch	Multi-plate, wet
Gear ratios:	4th	1.00:1

	3rd	1.171:1
	2nd	1.661:1
	1st	2.788:1
Wheelbase	51- in.	
Wheels:	Front	2.75x18
	Rear	3.00x18
Suspension:	Front	Telescopic fork
	Rear	Swingarm, dual shock
Weight	337 lb.	
Fuel capacity	(Info N/A)	
Oil capacity	1.8 qt.	
Fuel consumption	60 mpg average	
Top speed:	(CB72) 96 mph	
	(CB77) 99 mph	

Models: CB72/77

Hawk/Super Hawk

Collectibility	*****
Cruising speed	65/70 mph
Comfort of ride	***
Passenger accommodations	**
Reliability	***
Parts/Service availability	**

Text Comments:

The first modern Japanese sports motorcycle equipped with electric starter and 8-in. DLS brakes. The Super Hawk would give 500-650cc British-bikes a run for their money in the '60s and often outrun them. Roller ball-bearing engines would spin up to 10,000 rpm happily. The 250 versions are rare in the United States because of lack of displacement restrictions. Most collectors like the early models, with flat seat and handlebars.

Highly collectible and great fun to ride!

Specifications

Models: CR250M Elsinore

1973–74

Engine	2-stroke, air-cooled, single-cylinder, piston port
Bore x stroke	70x64.4 mm
Displacement	247.8cc (15 ci)
Lubrication	Pre-mix, transmission oil
Compression ratio	7.2:1
Horsepower	33 hp @ 7,500 rpm
Transmission	5-speed
Shift	Left side, return shift
Shift pattern	Down for low, 4 up from neutral

Primary drive	Gear-driven	
Clutch	Multi-plate, wet	
Gear ratios	[need info]	
Wheelbase	56.5-In.	
Wheels:	Front	3.00x21
	Rear	4.00x18
Suspension:	Front	Telescopic fork
	Rear	Swingarm, dual shocks
Curb weight	213 lb.	
Fuel capacity	7 liters (1.85 gal)	
Top speed:	(Info N/A)	

Model: CR250M Elsinore

Collectibility	*****
Cruising speed	Info N/A
Comfort of ride	***
Passenger acco mmodations	none
Reliability	***
Parts/Service availability	**

Text Comments:

Honda's first 2-stroke dirt racer (or 2-stroke racer of any kind). Light, fast with good handling out of the box. Motor overmatched the original frames, which needed reinforcing to keep from cracking the rear engine mounts. 250 Elsinores overwhelmed the 250cc classes and won all the marbles year after year. Still competitive in Vintage MX and also a desirable collectors bike.

Specifications

Model: GB500

1989–90

Engine	4-stroke, air-cooled, SOHC, 4-valve, single-cylinder	
Bore x stroke	92x75 mm (3.62x2.95-in.)	
Displacement	498 cc (30.4 ci)	
Lubrication	Dry-sump, pressure-fed	
Compression ratio	8.9:1	
Horsepower	40	
Transmission	5-speed	
Shift	Left side, return change	
Shift pattern	Down for low, 4 up from neutral	
Primary drive	Gear-driven	
Clutch	Multi-plate, wet	
Gear ratios:	5th	.875
	4th	1.00
	3rd	1.200
	2nd	1.555
	1st	2.384

Wheelbase	1412 mm (55.6-in.)	
Wheels	Alloy spoke rims	
Suspension:	Front	35 mm, telescopic fork
	Rear	Swingarm, dual shocks
Dry weight	359 lb.	
Saddle height	31.1-in.	
Fuel capacity	16.5 liters (4.4 gal)	
Fuel consumption	55 mpg average	
Top speed	105 mph	

Model GB500 "Tourist Trophy"

Collectibility	****
Cruising speed	70 mph
Comfort of ride	****
Passenger accommodations	none
Reliability	*****
Parts/Service availability	***

Text Comments:

Honda revives the "classic thumper look" with this XL/XR500 based engine in a fresh frame. Unbelievably smooth for a single (counterbalanced crankshaft), this 1950s-replica solo-seat, street bike looks and drives the part, without flinging oil and shaking all of the parts off. Beautiful styling, finish, and details! This nostalgic classic was only sold for two years, mostly due to high initial price and flat-line performance. They do respond well to some tweaks and mods, though. Bored to 600cc and given a cam, carburetor, and pipe . . . they turn into flyers!

Specifications

Model: GL1000 Gold Wing

1975–79

Engine	4-stroke, belt-driven SOHC, 8-valve, horizontally opposed, liquid-cooled, four-cylinder
Carburetion	(4) 32 mm
Bore x stroke	72x61.4 mm (2.834x2.417-in.)
Displacement	998cc (61 ci)
Lubrication	Pressure-fed, wet-sump
Compression ratio	9.2:1
Horsepower	85
Transmission	5-speed, constant-mesh
Shift	Left side, return change
Shift pattern	Down for low, 4 up from neutral
Primary drive	Gear-driven
Clutch	Wet, multi-plate

Gear ratios:	5th	.939:1
	4th	1.097:1
	3rd	1.333:1
	2nd	1.708:1
	1st	2.500:1
Wheelbase	60.8-in.	
Wheels	"Hollow-body" alloy, wire-spoke rims:	
Front	3.50x19-in.	
Rear	4.50x17-in.	
Suspension:	Front	Telescopic fork, nonadjustable damping
	Rear	Swingarm, incorporating drive shaft, dual shocks
Dry weight	583 lb.	
Saddle height	31.9-in.	
Fuel capacity	5.0 gal	
Oil capacity	4 qt.	
Fuel consumption	50 mpg average	
Top speed	125 mph (estimated)	

Model: GL1000 Gold Wing

Collectibility	*****
Cruising speed	75+ mph
Comfort of ride	****
Passenger accommodations	****
Reliability	*****
Parts/Service availability	***

Text Comments:

This Honda blockbuster machine launched thousands of touring adventures. The Gold Wing was Honda's first shaft-drive bike and first water-cooled, flat-four. Capable of 100 mph quarter-mile times, the performance was balanced with effortless ease on the highways. A fake "fuel tank" held storage and coolant overflow tank. The real fuel tank was under the seat!. Focus was on keeping a low center of gravity.

Wanna go coast-to-coast? This is your machine!

Specifications

Model: NT650 Hawk GT

1988–91

Engine	4-stroke,liquid-cooled 3-valve, SOHC V-twin
Bore x stroke	79x66 mm (3.11x2.60 ci)
Displacement	647cc (39.5 ci)
Lubrication	Pressure-fed, wet-sump

Compression ratio	9.4:1
Horsepower	(Info N/A)
Transmission	5-speed
Shift	Left-side, foot shift
Shift pattern	Down for low, 4 up from neutral
Primary drive	Gear-driven
Clutch	Multi-plate, wet
Gear ratios:	
	5th .996:1
	4th 1.174:1
	3rd 1.450:1
	2nd 1.882:1
	1st 2.769:1
Wheelbase	155 mm (56.3-in.)
Wheels:	Front 100/80x17-in.
	Rear150/70x17 in.
Suspension:	Front Telescopic
	Rear Single-sided swingarm, single shock
Weight	399 lb.
Fuel capacity	12 liters (3.17 gal)
Oil capacity	2.8 liters (3 qt.)
Fuel consumption	50 mpg average
Top speed	110 mph

Model: NT650 Hawk GT

Collectibility	****
Cruising speed	70 mph
Comfort of ride	****
Passenger accommodations	***
Reliability	*****
Parts/Service availability	****

Text Comments:

This beautiful 650 Sport Twin features a single-sided swingarm and an impressive 399 lb. dry weight. Honda made a swan from the ugly-duckling VT-500 Ascot twin. An all-around fun, smooth, great handling machine. Drawbacks: small fuel tank and forward sloping seat that puts you right up against the fuel tank.

Index